ELIZABETH I

ELIZABETH I

Ruler and Legend

CLARK HULSE

Published for The Newberry Library

UNIVERSITY OF ILLINOIS PRESS

Urbana and Chicago

© 2003 by The Newberry Library
All rights reserved
Manufactured in China
1 2 3 4 5 C P 5 4 3 2 1

Library of Congress Cataloging-in-Publication Data
Hulse, Clark, 1947–
Elizabeth I : ruler and legend / Clark Hulse.
p.   cm.
Includes bibliographical references.
ISBN 0-252-02893-7 (cl. : acid-free paper)
ISBN 0-252-07161-1 (pbk. : acid-free paper)
1. Elizabeth I, Queen of England, 1533–1603.
2. Great Britain—History—Elizabeth, 1558–1603.
3. Queens—Great Britain—Biography.
I. Title.
DA355.H86   2003
942.05'5'092—dc21   2003007106

CONTENTS

ILLUSTRATIONS

COLOR PLATES (*following page 40*)

TEXT FIGURES

PREFACE

This volume is a companion to the exhibitions organized by the Newberry Library and the American Library Association on the occasion of the four hundredth anniversary of the death of Elizabeth I of England.

No single exhibition can ever capture the complexity and continued fascination of Elizabeth. She lived her life in public and yet was in many ways highly secretive. Her image was spread far and wide, her life story the subject of eulogy and gossip, and yet her inner life remains largely unknown. We have many words from her own mouth and hand—speeches, letters, prayers, and poems—and yet each seems more like a performance than a revelation.

In order to bring this magnetic but elusive figure to as wide an audience as possible, the Newberry Library and the American Library Association have undertaken a unique collaboration that has resulted in not one but four exhibitions. The Newberry Library has assembled in Chicago a remarkable exhibition of more than a hundred rare books, manuscripts, maps, and other objects, on view at the library from September 30, 2003, through January 17, 2004. Most come from the Newberry's own rich collections. A loan of important manuscripts and maps from the British Library—many in Elizabeth's own hand—has made available materials rarely seen in America. The exhibition is further enriched with unique items from institutional and private collections in the Midwest, some never before seen by the public.

Simultaneously, the American Library Association has assembled a photographic exhibition of more than sixty of the most important items from the Newberry exhibition.

The American Library Association exhibition travels to forty American cities and towns in the nearly three-year period from October 2003 to March 2006.

Supplementing the Newberry and ALA exhibitions is a Web site, accessible at <http://www.newberry.org/elizabeth>. In addition to photographs and text derived from the Newberry and ALA exhibitions, the Web site contains supplemental images and educational materials. The unique qualities of the site allow the materials to be reorganized and understood in new ways.

Finally, this volume may be thought of as an exhibition in itself. Here the images from the Newberry and ALA exhibitions are woven into a narrative of Elizabeth's life and time. To put it another way, this volume attempts to tell her story through the objects. In doing so, it has two goals. For those who have seen the exhibitions, it allows a return visit at any time, to see again the books, portraits, maps, and manuscripts that survive among us from Elizabeth's time and Elizabeth's hand. For those who will not have a chance to see the exhibitions, this volume attempts to present the objects and let them speak. History often tells its story in too distant a voice. The materials of the past survive in many places, but often they are accessible to only a few. If they can be made to speak to us, then the voice of the past is lively in our ears.

ACKNOWLEDGMENTS

A project of this nature is possible only through the commitment of many institutions and through the dedicated work of many minds and hands.

First, we must thank the National Endowment for the Humanities for the major grants that made this project possible. Any views, findings, conclusions, or recommendations expressed in this catalogue do not necessarily reflect those of the NEH. The Illinois Humanities Council provided support for public programming.

Major support for the Newberry exhibition and catalog has been provided by William Vance and the Vance Family Fund, and by the University of Illinois at Chicago.

For their thoughtfulness and cooperation with loans, we are grateful to the British Library, especially Pamela Porter; the Spencer Research Library, University of Kansas, especially Richard Clement; and the Rare Book and Special Collections Library of the University of Illinois at Urbana-Champaign, especially Barbara Jones and Alvan Bregman. Particular thanks are due to Mr. and Mrs. John H. Bryan.

In her role as senior historical consultant, Carole Levin contributed her knowledge and intelligence at every stage. For their generous guidance, we are grateful to Janel Mueller, Leah Marcus, Mary Beth Rose, David Woodward, Mami Nagase, Georgianna Ziegler, Rachel Doggett, David Spence, and David Starkey.

At the Newberry Library, thanks are due to Charles Cullen, James Grossman, Mary Janzen, Riva Feshbach, Dina Kalman Spoerl, Susan Rusick, Joellen Dickie, Christine Colburn, Bob Karrow, Paul Gehl, Paul Saenger, John Powell, Catherine Gass, and Jessica Labatte. Carla Zecher, director of the Center for Renaissance Studies, has been a remarkable project director. At the American Library Association, Susan Brandehoff has provided expertise and experience.

At the University of Illinois at Chicago, the work of the curatorial team has been carried forward by three talented individuals: Jonathan Walker, Kristina Dziedzic, and Anna Riehl.

Carla Zecher has contributed to this book a commentary on music at the Tudor court, and Jonathan Walker has written the sidebar discussions of political survival in Tudor England, sixteenth-century European queens, Elizabeth as an Indian queen, and Elizabeth and the theater.

CHRONOLOGY

1509	Henry VIII becomes king of England, marries Katharine of Aragon, widow of his older brother, Arthur
1516	Queen Katharine gives birth to Mary Tudor
1517	Martin Luther begins Reformation at Wittenberg, Germany
1533	Henry VIII divorces Katharine of Aragon, marries Anne Boleyn, and breaks with Roman Catholic Church; Queen Anne Boleyn gives birth to Elizabeth Tudor (September 7)
1536	Queen Anne Boleyn is executed
1537	Queen Jane Seymour gives birth to Edward Tudor
1547	King Henry VIII dies; Edward VI becomes king
1553	King Edward VI dies; Mary Tudor becomes queen and restores Catholicism
1554	Sir Thomas Wyatt is executed; Elizabeth imprisoned; Mary I weds King Philip II of Spain
1558	Queen Mary I dies; Elizabeth Tudor becomes queen
1564	William Shakespeare is born in Stratford-upon-Avon
1566	James Stuart is born in Edinburgh
1568	Mary Queen of Scots takes refuge in England

1569–71	The Northern Rebellion in Yorkshire is suppressed
1570	Pope Pius V excommunicates Elizabeth
1572	Thomas Howard, duke of Norfolk, is executed; St. Bartholomew's Day Massacre in France
1577–80	Sir Francis Drake circumnavigates the globe
1579–81	François Hercule de Valois, duke of Anjou (also known as Alençon), visits Elizabeth to negotiate marriage
1584	Sir Walter Raleigh establishes "Virginia" colony, named for Queen Elizabeth, the Virgin Queen
1585	Queen Elizabeth sends army to intervene in the war in the Netherlands
1586	The Babington Plot, a conspiracy to assassinate Queen Elizabeth, is revealed
1587	Mary Queen of Scots is executed
1588	The English navy and foul weather defeat Philip II's Spanish Armada
1594	William Shakespeare and others form the Lord Chamberlain's Men
1601	Robert Devereux, earl of Essex, leads a rebellion and is executed; Queen Elizabeth addresses her last parliament
1603	Queen Elizabeth I dies (March 24); James VI of Scotland becomes James I of England

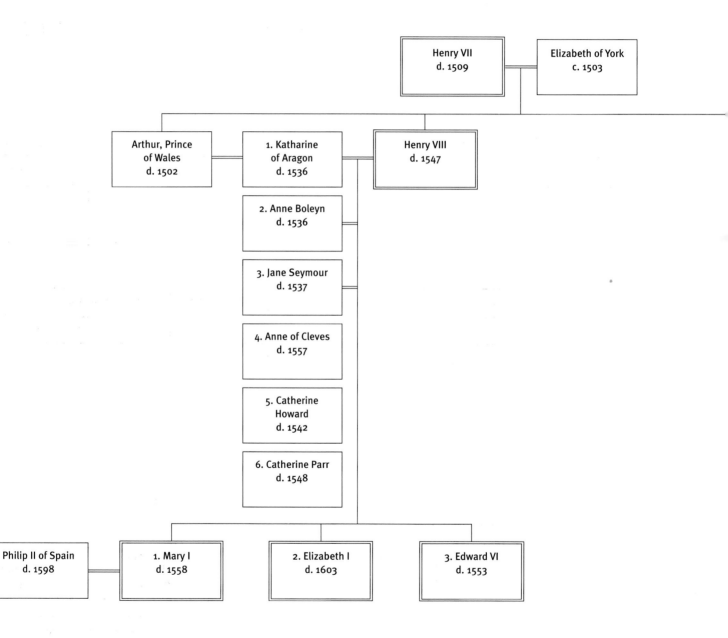

THE ROYAL HOUSE OF TUDOR

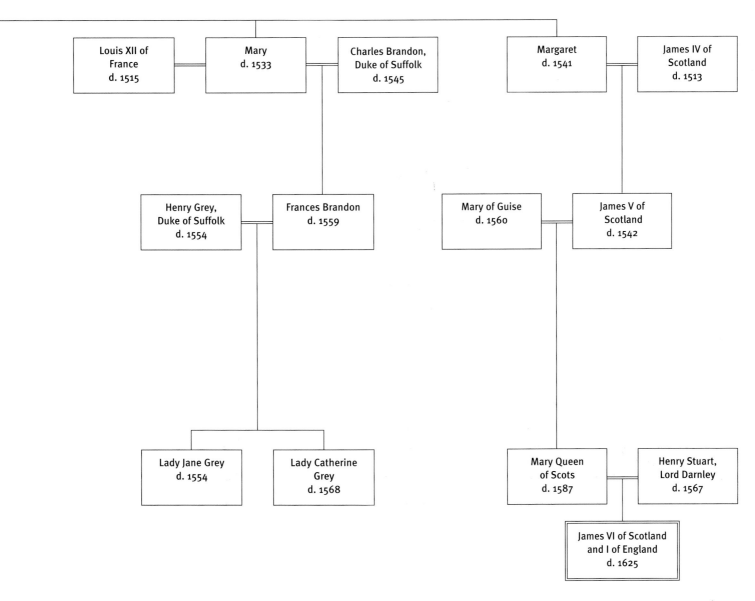

Louis XII of France d. 1515 — Mary d. 1533 — Charles Brandon, Duke of Suffolk d. 1545

Margaret d. 1541 — James IV of Scotland d. 1513

Henry Grey, Duke of Suffolk d. 1554 — Frances Brandon d. 1559

Mary of Guise d. 1560 — James V of Scotland d. 1542

Lady Jane Grey d. 1554

Lady Catherine Grey d. 1568

Mary Queen of Scots d. 1587 — Henry Stuart, Lord Darnley d. 1567

James VI of Scotland and I of England d. 1625

ELIZABETH I

DEATH AND BIRTH

On March 24, 1603, a great queen died. The historian William Camden, eighteen years younger than the queen herself, summed up her reign this way: "No oblivion shall smother her glory: For her most happy memory liveth, and so shall live in men's minds to all posterity." Her successor, James I, held that her wisdom as a monarch surpassed that of all rulers since the days of the great Augustus Caesar (figure 1).[1]

If the end was glorious, it was not altogether pretty. As Camden describes it, the queen began to feel weak during the winter and took sick at the end of January. As she grew more ill, those about her began, at first secretly and then more openly, to curry favor with James, who, as king of Scotland and the queen's own cousin, was expected to be her heir. By early March "a heavy dullness . . . familiar to old age, began to lay hold on her."[2]

She stopped eating, was lost in meditation, and would talk only with the archbishop of Canterbury, "until by little and little her speech failed her." A ring symbolizing her marriage to her kingdom was cut from her finger. Finally, as Camden tells it, when she was pressed to name her successor, she answered cryptically: "I will that a King succeed me: and who but my nearest kinsman, the king of Scots?"[3] The rest was silence.

Shrewd and subtle even in the weakness of death, Elizabeth Tudor had staged her final scene. Born on the Eve of the Nativity of the Virgin Mary, England's Virgin Queen slipped away on the Eve of the Annunciation of the Virgin Mary. The symbolism was not lost on Camden and his contemporaries. She was, concluded Camden, "called out of the

FIGURE 1. Francis Delaram, *Elizabeth I.* Frontispiece from William Camden, *Annales: The True and Royall History of the famous Empresse Elizabeth Queene of England France and Ireland* (London, 1625). Case F 4549 .137. Newberry Library, Chicago.

prison of her body unto an everlasting Country in heaven, most quietly departing this life, . . . in the 44th year of her reign, and of her age the 70th, unto which no King of England ever attained before."[4]

Elizabeth's skill as a ruler was the stuff of legend, and she somehow managed to weave even her own birth and death into that legend.

Elizabeth I of England was indeed one of those rare individuals who changed history from the moment of her birth. Her father, Henry VIII, broke with the Roman Catholic Church in order to marry his second wife, Anne Boleyn, and to legitimize their expected child. As a royal princess during the reigns of her brother and sister, the young Elizabeth was at the center of speculation, rumor, and even plots about the possibility that she too might eventually hold the scepter. As queen, she oversaw a period of breathtaking cultural achievement. She kept England from being torn apart by the wars of religion that raged on the European continent, and she withstood the massive military threat of the Spanish Armada.

Above and beyond the accomplishments of her reign, Elizabeth has captured and held popular imagination. To her supporters she was known as Gloriana and the Faerie Queene. According to her enemies, she was the ruthless supporter of a false religion; the murderer of her own cousin Mary Queen of Scots; a wanton and licentious woman, herself illegitimate, who spawned illegitimate children of her own with her numerous lovers and then disposed of the babies; a crowned coquette who dallied with her favorites at court while ignoring the poor sailors and soldiers who had preserved her kingdom.

Succeeding generations have largely sided with her supporters, admiring her political skill, her personal dignity, and her ability to overcome the obstacles facing a powerful woman in a world controlled by men. Even those who criticized her ends or her means have marveled at the cunning with which she pursued them. Elizabeth I is a subject of unabated interest to historians, novelists, and filmmakers, and is perhaps more famous now than in her lifetime, or at the time of her death. This may be neither an accident nor a trick of history. Both the good and the bad of her life and time speak to the present, because they resonate with our abiding concerns. What makes a person worthy to rule? How does the prospect or experience of supreme authority shape the person whom fate has chosen? What are the tolerable limits of debate and dissension within a state or nation? And how is the consciousness of a nation or a people formed out of those dissensions, rivalries, and threats, as well as from its commerce with others and the imprint of its charismatic leaders? In short, the questions that Elizabethans asked about their queen find their equivalents in questions we still ask, however great the differences of time and place.

Scena Quarta.

Enter Trumpets sounding : Then two Aldermen, L. Maior,
Garter, Cranmer, Duke of Norfolke with his Marshals
Staffe, Duke of Suffolke, two Noblemen, bearing great
standing Bowles for the Christening Guifts : Then foure
Noblemen bearing a Canopy, vnder which the Dutchesse of
Norfolke, Godmother, bearing the Childe richly habited in
a Mantle, &c. Traine borne by a Lady : Then followes
the Marchionesse Dorset , the other Godmother, and La-
dies. The Troope passe once about the Stage, and Gar-
ter speakes.

Gart. Heauen

From thy endlesse goodnesse, send prosperous life,
Long, and euer happie, to the high and Mighty
Princesse of England *Elizabeth.*

Flourish.   Enter King and Guard.

Cran. And to your Royall Grace, & the good Queen,
My Noble Partners, and my selfe thus pray
All comfort, ioy in this most gracious Lady,
Heauen euer laid vp to make Parents happy,
May hourely fall vpon ye.

Kin. Thanke you good Lord Archbishop :
What is her Name ?

Cran. *Elizabeth.*

The shaping of the legend of Elizabeth is nowhere more visible than in William Shakespeare's account of her birth. It comes in his play *The Famous History of the Life of Henry the Eight*, produced in 1613, ten years after Elizabeth's death and toward the very end of Shakespeare's career (figure 2). The final scene of the play opens with the baptism of the infant Elizabeth. Thomas Cranmer, archbishop of Canterbury and Elizabeth's godfather, utters a prophecy in the presence of the king her father and the assembled nobles:

> All princely graces . . .
> Shall still be doubled on her. Truth shall nurse her,
> Holy and heavenly thoughts still counsel her.
> She shall be loved and feared. Her own shall bless her;
> Her foes shake like a field of beaten corn,
> And hang their heads with sorrow. Good grows with her.
> In her days every man shall eat in safety
> Under his own vine what he plants, and sing
> The merry songs of peace to all his neighbours.
> God shall be truly known, and those about her
> From her shall read the perfect ways of honour.[5]

Though Shakespeare and his audience could still remember the reality of Elizabeth and her reign, it is here already completely replaced by the Elizabeth of legend. Indeed, even as we see the legend firmly established, the play suggests that the legend was in place from the moment of her birth and predated her years as a ruler. This is true at least in part, and it was Elizabeth herself who helped to forge the legend within her own lifetime. But always, we must remember, there is one thing more interesting than the clear outline of the legend, and that is the shadowy complexity of the ruler herself.

PRINCESS ELIZABETH

Shakespeare's confident description is written with the benefit of hindsight. But it is unlikely that Archbishop Cranmer said any such thing, for the birth of the princess in 1533 was, in a sense, a terrible mistake. Henry VIII wanted a son, and Anne Boleyn was eager to oblige. In late January 1533, she was two months pregnant and safely married to a dangerous king. It was absolutely necessary that the child be legitimate. Henry had a thirteen-year-old bastard son, named Henry Fitzroy, who might be put on the throne if there was no better alternative, but it would be a tricky business at best (and as it turned out, Fitzroy would die at age seventeen). The king's first wife, Queen Katharine of Aragon, was packed off to Cambridgeshire and closely watched. At court she was spoken of only in hushed voices as the "Princess Dowager of Wales," in reference to her prior marriage to Henry's deceased older brother, Arthur. The archbishop of Canterbury had given Henry the annulment from Katharine that the pope had refused. An elaborate coronation procession and ceremony for Anne included decorations by the great artist Hans Holbein. After years of tortuous maneuvering, the royal pair was ready to usher in a new order (figure 3).

The king of France sent a present to the new queen (figure 4). It was a small, exquisite manuscript poem entitled "Le Pasteur évangelique" [The evangelical shepherd] by the French poet Clement Marot, beautifully illuminated with Anne's new royal coat of arms and a Boleyn falcon wearing a crown and holding a scepter (figure 5). Anne had been brought up in the French court, and her personality was well known there. The

6

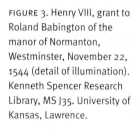

FIGURE 3. Henry VIII, grant to Roland Babington of the manor of Normanton, Westminster, November 22, 1544 (detail of illumination). Kenneth Spencer Research Library, MS J35. University of Kansas, Lawrence.

FIGURE 4. Francesco Bartolozzi, after Hans Holbein the Younger, *Anne Boleyn,* circa 1800. Engraving, 38.9 × 27.7 cm. Private collection.

FIGURE 5. Royal arms of Anne Boleyn, from Clement Marot, "Le Pasteur évangelique" [The evangelical shepherd], 1533. MS Royal 16 E. XIII. Reproduced by permission of the British Library.

FIGURE 6. Gentleman's embroidered nightcap, circa 1600. Red and green silk, silver-gilt thread, sequins, and gold lace on linen. Mr. and Mrs. John H. Bryan.

French king's gift can be described as a personal book, appealing to the new queen's reputation for learning and her commitment to religion. At the end, the great poet added verses just for the occasion, expressing his hope that "my lady Anne . . . queen incomparable" would have a son who was "the visible image / Of the king his father" and would reach the age of wisdom.[6] The queen's bed was her throne (figure 6).

As the day drew near, birth announcements from the queen were prepared. The date was left blank, to be filled in after the happy event, but confidently they announced the expected son (figure 7): "Where as it hath pleased the goodness of almighty god of his infinite mercy and grace to send unto us at this time good speed in the deliverance and bringing forth of a prince to the great joy, rejoice and inward comfort of my lord [the king] us [the queen] and of all his good and loving subjects of this his Realm." But the child was a girl, and so, in a different color ink, "prince" is changed to "princess," at the beginning and again at the end, when the queen asks for prayers "for the good health, prosperity and continual preservation of the said prince [changed to 'princess'] accordingly given under our signet at my lord's Manor of Greenwich this 7th day of September in the 25th year of my said lord's reign."[7]

So Henry did not get his son, at least not for another four years. Instead he got a second daughter, having already had Mary, now a seventeen-year-old girl, the child of the cast-off Katharine. Yet Elizabeth would, as Shakespeare's archbishop proclaimed, prove second to none. She would be far more her father's child than Henry could have had the wit to hope for. But there was perhaps a glimmer of hope for her future in her name, for Henry chose for her the name of another remarkable woman, his own mother—Elizabeth. Daughter of the last king of the House of York, Edward IV, she had married the last hope of the House of Lancaster, Henry, earl of Richmond. When Richmond's victory over Richard III put him on the throne as Henry VII, his marriage to Elizabeth of York joined the two houses into the new House of Tudor and put an end to the War of the Roses.

Princess Elizabeth was born into a royal court famous throughout Europe for its splendor and accomplishments. Henry VIII himself was proud of his learning. He had tried his hand at theology, though with mixed results. His refutation of Martin Luther won praise from the pope and the title of Defender of the Faith, but this was something of an embarrassment when Henry contested the authority of the pope. He consorted with men of accomplishment, such as the lyrical poet Sir Thomas Wyatt and the great scholar and writer Sir Thomas More, who had been his lord chancellor.

The king was also a skilled musician and composer. Foreign governments knew they could appeal to him through musical gifts, such as the richly illuminated part books of Italian songs presented to him by the Commune of Florence in 1527 (plate 1). With music

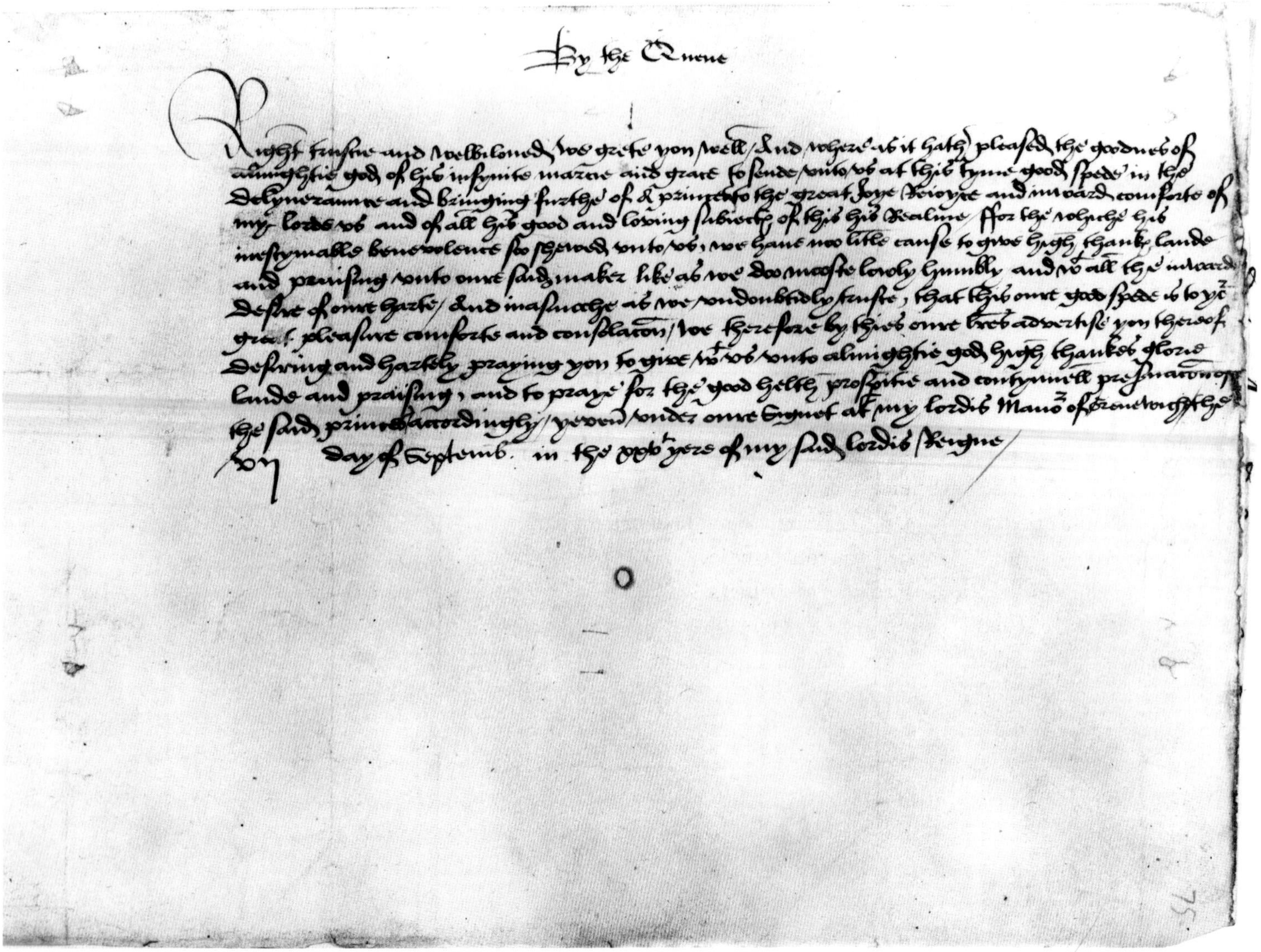
By the Quene

Right trustie and welbiloved we grete you well / And where as it hath pleased the goodnes of
almightie god of his infinite mercie and grace to sende unto us at this tyme good spede in the
delyveraunce and bringing furthe of a princes to the great joye rejoyse and inward comforte of
my lorde us and of all his good and loving subiects of this his Realme ffor the whiche his
inestymable benevolence so shewed unto us we have noo litle cause to give high thankes laude
and praising unto oure said maker like as we doo moste lowly humbly and with all the inward
desire of oure harte / And inasmuche as we undoubtedly truste that this oure good spede is to your
great pleasure comforte and consolacon / we therefore by thies oure lres advertise you thereof
desiring and hartely praying you to give with us unto almightie god high thankes glorie
laude and praising, and to praye for the good helthe prosperitie and contynuall preservacon of
the said princes accordingly / yeven under oure Signet at my lordis Manor of Grenewiche the
vij day of Septembr in the xxv yere of my said lordis Reigne

FIGURE 7. Birth announcement for a "princes," from Queen Anne Boleyn to George Brooke, Lord Cobham, September 7, 1533. MS Harley 283, fol. 75r. Reproduced by permission of the British Library.

and poetry went the splendid pageants and banquets of Henry's court, furnished with fine objects (plate 2).

It was also a court where women were expected to be well educated. Katharine of Aragon had been a great patron of humanists, including Erasmus and Juan Luis Vives. Anne Boleyn and Henry's sixth wife, Catherine Parr—with whom Elizabeth lived for several years—were interested in theology. The daughters of Sir Thomas More had won international renown for their learning. Elizabeth and her older sister, Mary, both were provided the best teachers and the best books.

We have the word of her tutor Roger Ascham that the princess Elizabeth was a good student, even, he thought, as good as a man. "Her mind has no womanly weakness, her perseverance is equal to that of a man, and her memory long keeps what it quickly picks up."[8] She studied the New Testament in Greek, as well as Sophocles and Aristotle. In Latin she read Cicero and Roman history.[9] After she was on the throne, Ascham recorded how he and the young queen would read together the Greek orations of Demosthenes. Elizabeth was especially proficient at languages and throughout her adulthood liked to show off her French and Italian as well as the classical languages. Some observers, though, politely suggested that her own opinion of her learning was a bit higher than her performance showed. In any event, she was an unusual pupil, and she received a remarkable education. It would prepare her to rule, if fortune smiled, or to be a patroness at some foreign court or country estate, if that was what fate held in store for her.

We can be sure that Elizabeth not only studied her books, she also studied her father, his speeches, his choice of advisors, and how he went about being king. She learned from him how to set policy and delegate its execution to able followers, and how to distance herself from bad results. From him she learned how to suspend her subjects between fear and love, though he inclined more to using fear as he grew older, and she always preferred to use love, unless fear was required.

In later life, Elizabeth's speeches to Parliament would echo her father's, especially his last or "Golden" speech. Usually the king sat silently during the opening or closing of a Parliament while the lord chancellor read or recited the king's words for him. (This is the reverse of the practice now, where the monarch reads the speech written for her by the prime minister.) But on December 24, 1545, at the conclusion of his last Parliament, Henry VIII himself spoke after the lord chancellor had finished. "I cannot choose but love and favor you," he said to the representatives of the people, "affirming that no prince in the world more favoreth his subjects than I do you, nor no subjects or commons more love and obey their sovereign lord than I perceive you do me." He went on to scold them for the religious dissent of the Reformation, but the overall effect, according to the chronicler Edward Hall, was marvelous. "This the king's oration was to his subjects there

Music at the Tudor Court

Elizabeth I took great pleasure in music, learned no doubt from her father. Henry played the harp and composed his own songs. Elizabeth is said to have played both the lute and the virginal, the two musical instruments considered appropriate for women in her day. (The term "virginal" was used in sixteenth-century England for all plucked keyboard instruments, like the later spinet.)

The Scottish ambassador Sir James Melville describes how he entered a chamber and heard the queen playing skillfully, but she left off as soon as she saw him. There can be no doubt that Elizabeth knew he was there and intended for him to hear her. But by demonstrating modesty she was heeding the advice offered by Baldassare Castiglione in his *Book of the Courtier* that women should be shy about musical performance and dancing. Elizabeth claimed to Melville that she wasn't used to playing in front of men, but that she played only when she was alone, to avoid melancholy. Yet she

is known to have performed for delegations of French ambassadors on at least two occasions.

Elizabeth employed an orchestra of about thirty instrumental musicians (including players of recorders, viols, violins, lutes, and keyboards), who played during her midday meal and for dancing. In her chapel, thirty-two gentleman singers and twelve choirboys performed sacred vocal works, music so lavish that one foreign visitor commented that the services held in the Chapel Royal were similar to those of the Roman Catholics. Indeed, the two premier Chapel composers, Thomas Tallis and his pupil William Byrd, were both secret Catholics whom Elizabeth retained in her service and protected because of their extraordinary talent.

In 1575, armed with a patent from the queen for the exclusive printing and marketing of all vocal music and lined music paper in England, Tallis and Byrd issued a volume of their own vocal compositions in Latin (figure 8). The title of the collection,

FIGURE 8. "De Anglorum Musica" [On English music], from Thomas Tallis and William Byrd, *Cantiones, quae ab argumento sacrae vocantur* [Songs called sacred because of their texts] (London, 1575). Case -VM 2099 L63 T14c. Newberry Library, Chicago.

FIGURE 9. "Byrd's Lullaby," from William Byrd, *Psalmes, sonets, & songs of sadnes and pietie* (London, circa 1590). Case -VM 1579 .B99p. Newberry Library, Chicago.

Cantiones, quae ab argumento sacrae vocantur [Songs called sacred because of their texts], hints that the composers were nervous that the music might seem more appropriate for Catholic worship than for the English church. Elizabeth had not forbidden the use of Latin church music, and the book was dedicated to her. If she had disapproved, it would not have seen print. But the *Cantiones* venture was not a commercial success.

Byrd clearly learned his lesson, for he waited over a decade before making another attempt at music publishing. Tallis had died, leaving Byrd sole possessor of the patent. Byrd's next collection bore an English title (*Psalmes, sonets, & songes*) and contained lyrics entirely in English (figure 9). The "Lullaby" to the infant Christ became famous, combining religious significance with native English charm. This songbook quickly sold out, and two more editions followed in quick succession. The patent that Elizabeth had given to Tallis and Byrd "for the especiall affection and good will that we have and bear to the science of music and for the advancement thereof" had at last borne fruit.

—Carla Zecher

The Education of Elizabethan Women

Elizabeth grew up in a period in which the humanist values of learning were extended to girls and young women, at least within the social elite. In 1561, Sir Thomas Hoby wrote in his translation of *The Courtier* by Baldassare Castiglione that "You shall find that continually virtue hath reigned as well among women as men: and that such there have been also that have made war and obtained glorious victories, governed realms with great wisdom and justice, and done whatever men have done."[1]

Like most girls who were educated, Elizabeth shared her early instruction with her brother, Edward, and was later provided with tutors of her own: first William Grindal and then Roger Ascham. Her sister, Mary Tudor, had likewise received a fine education as the first legitimate child of Henry VIII. Mary's mother, Katharine of Aragon, had commissioned a plan for her education from the leading Spanish humanist, Juan Luis Vives, which was published in 1523 as *The Instruction of a Christen Woman*. Their cousin Lady Jane Grey, who was tutored by her family's chaplain, John Aylmer, distinguished herself in her studies even beyond her parents' wishes, since they were more interested in preparing her for the stylish life of court than for sober academic contemplation. And the erudite reputation of Margaret More (later Roper), one of Sir Thomas More's daughters, spread throughout the learned circles of Europe.

As notable as the intellectual achievements of these women might be, the opportunities for formal education for girls and young women rarely extended beyond these elite circles. Young women were not admitted to the institutions in which young men received formal educations, such as the universities at Oxford or Cambridge, or the Inns of Court in London, where lawyers were trained. Only occasionally did girls attend grammar schools at the elementary level. In his 1581 book on education, *Positions,* even the progressive humanist teacher Richard Mulcaster wrote that education for women was only an "accessory."[2]

Despite these obstacles to formal education, Elizabethan women achieved great things, many of which have come to light only in recent years. Mary Herbert, countess of Pembroke (and sister to the poet Sir Philip Sidney), was the leading literary patron of the age. Her daughter, Lady Mary Wroth, was a fine poet, as was the gentlewoman Amelia Lanyer. In 1589, one Jane Seagar wrote a visionary book entitled *Prophecies of the Ten Sibyls* and dedicated it to Elizabeth. Esther Inglish (or Inglis) created beautiful calligraphy books, written in a fine italic hand and decorated in a style that recalled the great illuminated manuscripts produced at Bruges and Ghent a century before. Frequently they are dedicated to noblewomen and gentlewomen who themselves were devoted to learning. One of Inglish's books presented to Lady Arskese of Dirltoun in 1606 gives examples of the author's "handwriting and limning" (miniature painting), and Inglish notes in the dedication that had she realized that Lady Arskese knew French, she would have written it in that language (plate 4).

Above all, the availability of the Bible in English gave women in every parish both the materials and the motive for learning to read. Then as now, education had practical purposes beyond the cultivation of the intellect or the spirit. Later in life, Elizabeth talked about how she had studied theology in her youth but had turned to the study of history and government when she came to the throne.[3] Other women might not have kingdoms to run, but depending on their social status, they might have manor houses or small businesses to operate while their husbands were at court or on the shop floor. In such unofficial positions, they would need basic literacy, plus skills in mathematics. These were learned from fathers, mothers, and brothers, in the home or on the job.

One historian has estimated that in 1500, only 1 or 2 percent of women in England were literate, but a century later it was 10 percent.[4] The number was only to grow.

NOTES

1. Sir Thomas Hoby, *The Courtyer of Count Baldessar Castilio* (London, 1561), fol. Cc3v.
2. Richard Mulcaster, *Positions wherin those primitive circumstances be examined, which are necessarie for the training up of children, wither for skill in their booke, or health in their bodie* (London, 1581), p. 133.
3. Leah S. Marcus, Janel Mueller, and Mary Beth Rose, eds., *Elizabeth I: Collected Works* (Chicago: University of Chicago Press, 2000), p. 96.
4. David Cressy, *Literacy and the Social Order: Reading and Writing in Tudor and Stuart England* (Cambridge: Cambridge University Press, 1980), p. 177.

present such comfort that the like joy could not be unto them in this world."[10] Elizabeth was fourteen at the time of this storied event, and from it she learned how powerful the personal touch of a monarch can be, and how important it is to promise love and favor, when what you want in return is love and obedience.

In her father's last years, Princess Elizabeth must also have studied the king's courtiers, since she was herself, in a sense, one of them. Like them, she depended on the king for her livelihood, her future hopes, and indeed her life. She must have watched as the nobles and officials of the realm did whatever was required to please him, even as they waited for him to die. And she must have watched them squirm and scramble as first her brother and next her sister came to the throne and then left it empty.

It was in this dangerous school that the princess Elizabeth learned what it meant to be a ruler, and what it meant to please or anger the ruler. She fashioned her own rule above all on that of her father, and his voice is like an instrument in the background of her speeches. But she knew too for many reasons that she could not be him, and shouldn't be if she could. For she had seen him send men to their deaths—and women, including her own mother—for slender or imagined crimes. She had seen him be wasteful in war and profligate in peace, hated by the weak and feared by the wise. Sir Robert Naunton cited Henry's nature if not his words when he claimed that Henry had once boasted about never sparing any man in his anger, nor any woman in his lust.[11] Elizabeth wanted to possess her father's courage and cleverness, but not his anger and lust.

The similarity of father and daughter, and the difference, is captured in two seals, used for official documents. On the fronts of their respective seals, Elizabeth and her father are seated on their thrones, holding the orb and scepter, and facing down the viewer. On the back of his seal, Henry is mounted on horseback in full armor, charging

FIGURE 10. Henry VIII, grant to Roland Babington of the manor of Normanton, Westminster, November 22, 1544 (detail of Great Seal). Kenneth Spencer Research Library, MS J35. University of Kansas, Lawrence.

FIGURE 11. Elizabeth I, appointment of Edward North as Lord Lieutenant of Cambridgeshire and the Isle of Ely, May 1, 1559 (detail of Great Seal). Kenneth Spencer Research Library, MS J36. University of Kansas, Lawrence.

with his lance (figure 10). Never mind that he was in his fifties and too hefty to get on a horse anymore; the official image shows his vigor and potency and refusal to grow old gracefully. On the back of the other seal, Elizabeth by contrast is seated sedately on her palfrey (figure 11). She is on horseback—after all, the monarch, whether male or female, must command the military—but her pace is measured and steady, governed by intelligence and a determination to endure.

If Elizabeth had an ambivalent identification with her father, she had an even more complex identification with her mother. Elizabeth owned a diamond ring that opened to show enamels of herself and her mother facing each other.[12] She would become furious with those who made reference to her mother's execution. Elizabeth and Anne shared the same motto: "Semper eadem"—"always the same." On the surface it meant that one did not change one's mind or one's character to suit the occasion. In this case it may have also suggested that mother and daughter were the same. But by and large, Anne Boleyn was a subject that Elizabeth didn't talk about.

Even for a princess, Elizabeth had a childhood like no other. At her birth, she was her father's heir. Four years later, she was declared illegitimate when her baby brother, Edward, was born. Henry VIII at his death in 1547 disposed of the kingdom in his will—a novel arrangement, since the realm was hardly private property. First it would go to the boy

Forms of Identity

Today we define personal identity in many ways. Family, ethnicity, and nationality may each contribute to our sense of who we are. So do our personal experiences, our sense of an inner self, and the complex chemistry of our brains.

People in sixteenth-century England had their own ways of defining identity. For most, identity was a matter of family, occupation, and location. You stayed in your village or neighborhood, worked in the family trade, and found a spouse from among those who were acceptable to your parents.

For the aristocrats and gentlefolk, there were highly formalized systems to define social classes and family heritages, and to locate specific individuals within this class system. In his "Armorial bearings of kings and noble families" (1572), a manuscript book of heraldry commissioned by the Elizabethan military leader Sir Peregrine Bertie, Robert Cooke illustrates Elizabeth's identity through family genealogy. Cooke traces the descent of the queen's eminent ancestors, concluding with a full-page display of Elizabeth's elaborate coat of arms (plate 3). The fleurs-de-lys on the central shield represent her claim to the title "Queen of France," derived from Henry V, while the harp on the shield to the left represents her claim to Ireland. The Tudor roses recall the union of the houses of Lancaster (red rose) and York (white rose) in the marriage of her grandparents Henry of Richmond and Elizabeth of York. The motto "Honi Soit Qui Mal y Pense" [Evil to him who thinks evil] surrounding the shield symbolized her position as head of the Order of the Garter, which included aristocrats and foreign princes. And finally, the crown at the top marks her position as ruler.

The Latin motto "Semper eadem" [Always the same] that Elizabeth sometimes used suggests a second form of identity, based on personal characteristics or attitudes. Geoffrey Whitney's *A Choice of Emblems* (1586) offers a highly influential model for defining identity through moral and ethical characteristics. The volume depicts individuals in the midst of various crises. Their responses—whether right or wrong—to those crises are captured in short verses that interpret the images and guide the reader in his or her own ethical behavior. Andrea Alciato's *Emblemata* (1531), the forerunner to Whitney's *A Choice of Emblems,* was one of the most popular books of the century throughout Europe.

Finally, our identities might lie not in our families or ourselves, but in the stars. In treatises on astrology, a reader could find horoscopes not only for persons of great birth, such as Henry VIII, but also for men of great accomplishment, such as John Cheke and Albrecht Dürer. A chart for Elizabeth published in 1583 is based on the position of the stars at the moment of her birth in the thirty-sixth minute of the fourth hour of the seventh day of September 1533 (figure 12). These diverse ways of defining personal traits demonstrate that many of the terms by which we debate the nature of identity today have their analogs in Elizabeth's own time.

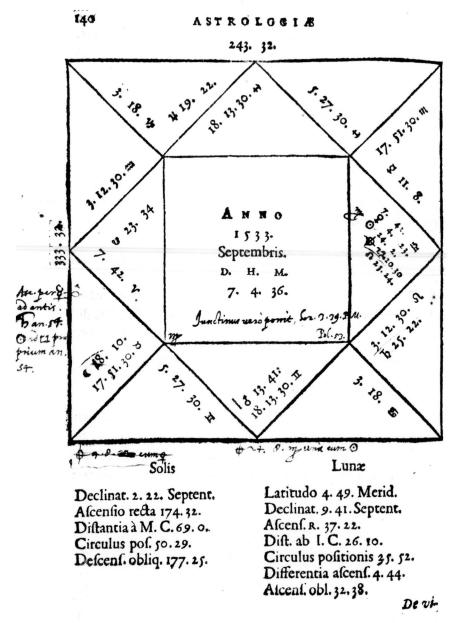

FIGURE 12. Astrological chart for Elizabeth I, from Sixtus ab Hemminga, *Astrologiæ* (Antwerp, 1583). Case B8635 .386, p. 140. Newberry Library, Chicago.

Edward, then to the girls in birth order: first the child of Katharine of Aragon, then the child of Anne Boleyn. Elizabeth was back in the line of succession, but had fallen to third place.

Elizabeth's position was an awkward third place at best. Edward's government was controlled by his uncle, Edward Seymour, duke of Somerset, who was the oldest brother of the young king's mother, Jane Seymour. Somerset as lord protector led a government that was strongly Protestant, and hence Elizabeth was more in its favor than was the Catholic Mary. But Somerset had a rival in his younger brother, Thomas Seymour, who began to play a dangerous game with Elizabeth as its object. King Edward was in poor health. If Thomas Seymour was to marry the fifteen-year-old princess, and the young king was to die, then Seymour could use Elizabeth to supplant both Mary and his own older brother Edward, the lord protector.

The game came to a head in 1549. Seymour was arrested for treason. Elizabeth's servants were taken to the Tower of London for interrogation and pressured to implicate their mistress, if only to save their own skins. Elizabeth herself was cut off from her brother and kept under close watch at Hatfield House. In her letters to the lord protector and the Privy Council (consisting of the monarch's "privy" or private advisors), Elizabeth was alternately pleading and defiant. Upset at rumors that she was pregnant by Seymour, she offered to come to court so that "I may show myself there as I am" to the king and council.[13] The stakes here were high. If she was indeed pregnant, that fact could itself be treason, since it would constitute an unauthorized tampering with the royal bloodline. It would make her unfit for marriage to a foreign prince or king. And it would confirm the beliefs of those who had hated her mother.

Receiving no answer from the lord protector or council, three weeks later Princess Elizabeth wrote again, demanding that the rumors be suppressed. She admits that the lord protector thinks she is too "well assured of mine own self" for one so young—and for a woman at that—and that "I take upon me to rule myself." Undeterred, she expresses her confidence that the council will do the right thing, both for Elizabeth's sake and so that the council can show its duty to a king whose sister has been slandered.[14]

The closing of the letter is both humble and threatening, as she signs herself "Your assured friend to my little power, Elizabeth" (figure 13). The decorative squiggle at the bottom right bears a remarkable resemblance to her father's way of signing. The firm, flourished signature itself presages the distinctive "Elizabeth" she would use when she came to the throne, with the squiggle replaced by "R" (for "regina," queen). What she was saying to the lord protector is clear: "be nice to me when I have little power, and I may indeed be your friend when I have great power." In the end, Seymour was sent to the block and executed, and Elizabeth seems to have gotten the rumors suppressed. It was a remarkable high-wire performance for a fifteen-year-old.

that you saye that I giue folkes occasion to thinke in refusinge the good to
vpholde the inel I am not of so simple vnderstandinge, nor I wolde that
your grace shulde haue so inel a opinion of me that I haue so litel respecte
to my none honestie that I wolde mainteine it if I had sonficiente promis
of the same, and so your grace shal proue me whan it comes to the pointe .
And thus I bid you farewel, desiringe god alwais to assiste you in al your
affaires . Writen in hast . Frome Hatfelde this 21 of Februarye .

Your assured frende to my litel
power Elizabeth

Elizabeth's own relations with her older sister, Mary, were polite and even some-times cordial, and she seems to have had a special affection for her brother the king. A few months after the Seymour affair, Elizabeth sent her portrait to Edward with a grace-ful letter (plate 5). She tells him that the portrait is a record only of her outward appear-ance. Far better it would be if it could show the "inward good mind" that Elizabeth bears toward him. Although the painted face may age or weather or be marred by accident, her mind will always be constant toward him in her love and regard. And if the portrait is where he can see it while she herself is absent, that simply expresses her desire to be with him more often.[15]

These are conventional things to say about portraits in the Renaissance, but the princess Elizabeth says them extremely well. The gift and letter show that she has learned her school lessons well, and has learned how to use her studies in her personal and po-litical interactions. And the fact that they are standard things to say does not mean that they are not true. The idea of constancy expressed in Elizabeth's motto "Semper eadem" lingers behind her letter to her brother. Her mind, her affections, her direction will not alter, no matter what happens, and no matter what outward appearances may suggest. The inner conscience and resoluteness of the future ruler are already set in the character of the teenager.

Around this same time, Elizabeth became very concerned about her personal ap-pearance. As a child, alternately in and out of favor with her father, she had sometimes lacked the proper wardrobe for a princess. In her early teen years, she liked to dress nicely, and in the portrait she sent to Edward, showing her at age thirteen, she wears a beautiful red dress trimmed in jewels, with a damasked gold undergarment, and pearls at her neck and on her cap. Still the overall impression is of a certain control, even se-verity, as her hair is neatly tucked in, her mouth firmly set, and her hands gently hold-ing a prayer book. Perhaps because of the rumors about her sexual behavior, she empha-sized the conservative—even puritanical—aspects of her appearance, in contrast to the more coiffured and bejeweled ladies of the courts of Edward and Mary. In November 1551, the Princess Mary sent her young cousin Lady Jane Grey a fine dress of gold cloth to wear to a diplomatic gala. But Jane refused it since she wanted to model herself on the plain style of her other cousin Elizabeth. "Nay . . . that were a shame to follow my lady Mary against God's word, and leave my lady Elizabeth, which followeth God's word."[16] This not only insulted Mary but was later quite ironic, since Elizabeth dressed gorgeously after she became queen and was angry with preachers who demanded that women dress in simple fashion.

On July 6, 1553, Edward died, setting off a whirlwind of events. John Dudley, duke of Northumberland, had succeeded Edward Seymour as lord protector and led a faction of the Privy Council in what amounted to a coup d'etat. Again Henry VIII's daughters—Mary as well as Elizabeth—were declared illegitimate, and the council looked to the descendants of Henry VIII's younger sister Mary for a queen. They found her in Mary's granddaughter, Lady Jane Grey, who was conveniently married to Dudley's son. But while the group had a queen, it didn't have the whole-hearted support of the people or even of the entire council. Mary herself escaped, having been tipped off by a member of the council, Henry Fitzalan, twelfth earl of Arundel. Within nine days, the coup collapsed, and Mary triumphantly entered London as queen.

The desperate nature of the nine-day reign of Lady Jane Grey is captured in the proclamation that she sent to leaders of the realm. As she claims the throne, she defends her reign against "the feigned and untrue claim of the Lady Mary, bastard daughter to our great uncle Henry the eighth of famous memory." At the bottom of the document we are told, in imperious form, that it is "Signed at our Tower of London the tenth July the first year of our reign." The first, last, and only. Jane would spend most of her remaining seven months of life in that same tower, and would be executed there. At the top of the page is Jane's teen-age signature, "Jane the queen" (figure 14). At some later point, the proclamation came into the possession of Elizabeth's chief minister, William Cecil, Lord Burghley, and he wrote on the back in grim humor, *Jana non regina—*"Jane *not* the queen."[17]

Mary reigned for a little over five years (figure 15). They were shaky years, marked by plots and rebellions, tortures and executions, including three hundred of her own subjects burned to death as heretics. As a result, Mary Tudor has gone down in history as "Bloody Mary." No one has argued that Mary was a particularly brilliant queen, but she was not an unusually bad one either, by the standards of the position. She may not have killed more people, per year, than other monarchs. And her basic policies made a great deal of sense. England would be restored to its customary rulers, in the persons of the eldest child of Henry VIII and the great nobles such as Cardinal Pole, the duke of Norfolk, and the earl of Arundel. English religion would be restored to its traditional liturgy and its fealty to Rome, which had guided it for centuries. English foreign policy would be restored to its traditional alignment with the Hapsburg dynasty that ruled Spain, the Netherlands, and much of central Europe. After all, Mary's ancestor John of Gaunt had married a Spaniard, as had her father, Henry VIII. So Mary wedded her mother's great-nephew, Prince Philip of Spain (soon to become King Philip II). Among the many works executed to commemorate their union was the magnificent "Queen Mary Atlas," showing the adjacent lands of England and Spain, separated only by narrow seas, and surmounted by the quartered arms of the two kingdoms (figure 16).

Mary's failings were not due to bad policies, but to bad timing. She came to the

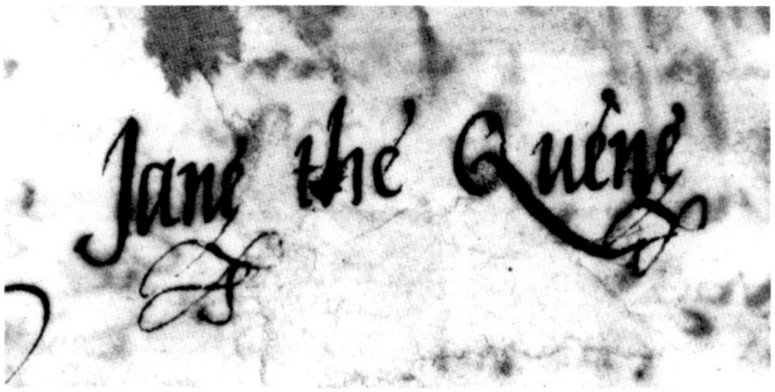

FIGURE 14. Queen Jane [Grey], letter to William Parr, Marquis of Northampton, July 10, 1553 (detail). MS Lansdowne 1236, item 15, fol. 24r. Reproduced by permission of the British Library.

FIGURE 15. Antonis Mor, *Queen Mary Tudor of England,* circa 1554. Oil on panel, 109 × 84 cm. Isabella Stewart Gardner Museum, Boston.

So You Want to Be a Monarch

People accustomed to the messiness of democratic government sometimes think monarchies run smoothly: each king is followed in turn by his son, or occasionally his daughter, and any possible deviation is greeted with horror by the loyal subjects of the realm.

Nothing could be farther from the experience of most people living under monarchies. Kings may die young, or have idiot children or no children at all. Powerful rivals may grasp the throne by force. In short, things happen.

This was certainly the case for the English people in the fifteenth and sixteenth centuries, as readers of Shakespeare's history plays know well. Between 1399 and 1603, thirteen people claimed the throne of England. Only *one* of them was an adult male inheriting the kingdom from his father. And that one, Henry V (Shakespeare's Prince Hal), had a bad reputation and looked at the outset like a sorry bet.

Henry IV	1399	Age 32	Usurped throne from cousin
Henry V	1413	Age 25	Inherited throne from father
Henry VI	1422	Age 9 mo.	Inherited throne from father
Edward IV	1461	Age 18	Usurped throne from cousin
Edward V	1483	Age 13	Inherited throne from father
Richard III	1483	Age 32	Usurped throne from nephew
Henry VII	1485	Age 28	Usurped throne from cousin
Henry VIII	1509	Age 18	Inherited throne from father
Edward VI	1547	Age 9	Inherited throne from father
Jane	1553	Age 15	Usurped throne from cousin
Mary I	1553	Age 37	Inherited throne from brother
Elizabeth I	1558	Age 25	Inherited throne from sister
James I	1603	Age 36	Inherited throne from cousin

throne too late to have children, though she tried. Many of the chief supporters of her regime, such as Cardinal Pole and Bishop Gardiner, were too old to see it through. Her husband was too young to have much interest in her. And England was perhaps too far gone down the road of reformation to be called back all the way.

Mary also suffered from a bad choice of enemies. Elizabeth proved to be less honest but much more clever than she, just as Anne Boleyn had been less honest but more clever than Katharine of Aragon. And among the radical Protestant exiles were brilliant propagandists such as John Foxe, whose history of the English Reformation, published from his place of refuge in Switzerland, created the legend of Mary as a bloodthirsty tyrant.[18]

Elizabeth's own life during this period is itself the material of legend. The celebration of her birth might be called the first legend of Elizabeth, as a child of destiny. The

FIGURE 16. "Occidens," from Diego Homem, "Queen Mary Atlas," 1558. MS Additional 5415A, fols. 9v–10r. Reproduced by permission of the British Library.

rumors about the princess and Seymour might be called the second, darker legend of Elizabeth, as a sexually precocious risk-taker. Elizabeth's dangers and amazing escapes during the time of Mary quickly became the subject of a third and more enduring legend. Elizabeth's enemies among Mary's court portrayed her as a two-faced schemer, immersed in plots to depose and murder Mary, even as she protested her loyalty to Mary and the Catholic Church. Elizabeth went to the Tower, and from the Tower to house arrest, at Mary's direct order. John Foxe devoted the entire concluding section of the *Actes and Monuments* to an account of "The Miraculous Preservation of the Lady Elizabeth, now Queen of England." And for years after her death, her youthful perils would be recorded in a succession of popular books, such as Thomas Heywood's *If you know not me, You know no bodie: Or, The troubles of Queene Elizabeth* (1613) (figure 17).

This third legend of Elizabeth, as one saved either by God or by her own cleverness, was created not only by those who wanted her out of the way or those who had pinned their hopes on her. It was created in large part by Elizabeth herself. She was knee-deep in the plots against Mary, or at least willing to allow her servants to be. She was in peril of assassination, or else gave out that she was. She was loyal and Catholic, or at least went through the outward motions. She was inwardly and secretly Protestant, or at least hinted at it. She knew that by the turn of a hair she could be queen or she could be dead. Above all, she knew that time was on her side, since Mary was seventeen years older. If she could stay alive, and Mary remained childless, then eventually Elizabeth would win. It was a unique historical position, incomprehensible to anyone who did not go through it.

Elizabeth knew her position was singular, and she later would lecture Parliament about it when it asked that she name a successor:

> I am sure there was not one of them [in Parliament] that ever was a second person [next in line to the throne], as I have been, and have tasted of the practices against my sister, who I would to God were alive again. I had great occasions to hearken to their motions, of whom some of them are of the Common House. But when friends fall out truth doth appear, according to the old proverb, and were it not for my honor, their knavery should be known. There were occasions in me at that time: I stood in danger of my life, my sister was so incensed against me. I did differ from her in religion and I was sought for divers ways, and so shall never be my successor.[19]

Her words are as cryptic as her actions had been. But roughly she is saying that "when I was heir to the throne, conspirators sought to use me to depose Mary. I had good reason to listen to them, since my life was in danger from my sister's anger over matters of religion, but I didn't. Some of those old conspirators are even now (in 1566) sitting in the House of Commons, and I could expose them, but I won't. When you are second

If yon knovv not me,
You know no bodie :
Or,
The troubles of Queene ELIZABETH:

At LONDON.
Printed for Nathaniell Butter. 1613.

FIGURE 17. Title page from Thomas Heywood, *If you know not me, You know no bodie: Or, The troubles of Queene Elizabeth* (London, 1613). Case 4A .881. Newberry Library, Chicago.

27

in line, people come at you from all sides, and for their own motives, and I am never going to put somebody else in that position. Indeed, if I named a successor, some of the people in this room might immediately try to manipulate that person in order to depose me."

The great irony of this little speech, of course, is that Elizabeth tells us just enough to let us know that she won't tell us everything. She tells us that she knows the secrets of others and has a few secrets of her own, and will continue to keep them. "Video et taceo" was one of her mottos: "I see and am silent," or even better, "I know everything and let slip nothing." By hinting at what she is not going to tell us, she reveals how she wants others to see her: intelligent, subtle, not easily fooled. Years earlier, in her teen-age letter to Protector Somerset, she had asked, "do you think me so simple" as not to see what others are up to? It is a phrase that occurs again and again in her letters and speeches. "Do you think I'm some sort of fool?" The Elizabeth who emerges from her sister's shadow is more than a little proud of her skills: her shrewd judgment of others; her ability to keep a secret; and above all, her ability to survive.

THE THRONE

On November 17, 1558, just before dawn, Elizabeth Tudor inherited the realm of England from her sister (plate 6). But what did she inherit?

The economy was in a recession. The government was broke. The people were divided over religion and had a bad impression of women rulers. The ruling class of nobles and knights was experienced in conspiracy and rebellion. Two powerful neighbors, France and Spain, alternately threatened, and France had an ally to the north in Scotland, while Spain had an ally across the Channel in the Netherlands.

On the other hand, Elizabeth had the good will of the people, astutely cultivated during her time of troubles. She had a loyal inner circle of highly capable advisors. She had few equals in the art of conspiracy. France and Spain could be played against each other. Religion could unite as well as divide.

England itself was a small nation, with a population of about three million. Most people had no vote and no formal say in government, though popular opinion could be a powerful influence on the behavior of the ruling elite. That elite itself was tiny: one monarch, a dozen or so major royal officers, about sixty aristocrats or "lords temporal" (dukes, earls, barons, and so forth), twenty-eight "lords spiritual" (archbishops, bishops, and abbots of the church), just under four hundred elected members of the House of Commons, and sundry knights and gentlemen. So the elite itself amounted to less than one-tenth of 1 percent of the population. Each of them came with a family, though, and so England was not just a pyramid with a tiny group at the top. It was also a series of spider webs, radiating out from each powerful person, and comprised of brothers, sisters, in-laws, cousins, distant relations, friends, and clients. It was through this network that England was really governed.

Coming to the throne, Elizabeth faced four immediate challenges: to put together a stable government, settle the religious question, find a safe path in foreign relations, and provide for the succession after her death. The first she did quickly. The second and third would occupy her for the next thirty years. The last she refused to do, ever.

Governments don't just happen. For a government to take power and hold power, it needs careful planning, the right people, quick and decisive action, and a large dose of good luck. In Mary's last days, Elizabeth had to conceal from Mary the mere fact that she had any plans. But the sequence of events proves that she indeed was ready. In her first months, Elizabeth built a council able actually to manage the government. She staged public ceremonies that rallied public opinion behind her. She acted to stabilize the economy. And—by her own actions and through her supporters—she carefully addressed the questions that lingered in many minds about whether women should be allowed to rule at all.

Forming a council was a balancing act. Aristocrats expected to be part of the regime just because of their birth, and they expected to be free to act in self-interest. But Elizabeth, like her father, also wanted men of ability, regardless of birth, who could run things efficiently and in her interests. A significant number of the aristocrats and councilors in her sister's day had been opposed to the idea of Elizabeth's ever being queen, and they might still join into an opposition party. Elizabeth, from the moment she learned she was queen, sought to get the government she wanted without giving ammunition to her enemies.

So Elizabeth carefully planned the stages by which she would take power. She did not go immediately to London from Hatfield House, where she had been kept under close watch during Mary's last days. Instead, she took several days to consolidate her hold on power before entering the capital. At some point in that period (historians differ about which day it was, so rapid was the pace of events), the new monarch met with the old Privy Council. She added to the council her chief loyalists, especially William Cecil (later Lord Burghley), who would be her principal advisor for forty years. She kept the leading nobles on the council, both because she had to and because that way she could keep her eye on them. She retained the most experienced figures from the governments of her father and brother. But she dismissed many from her sister's time, saying that she required of them "nothing more but faithful hearts," and telling them that it was only because a larger group would "make rather discord and confusion than good counsel."[20] In a stroke, she put her people in place and pacified her opponents.

Elizabeth's England

When Henry VII, the first Tudor king, ended the War of the Roses with his victory at Bosworth in 1485, the kingdom that he won was largely feudal, rural, and agricultural. The kingdom that his granddaughter left at her death in 1603 was more modern, more urban, and more commercial.

William Cuningham's beautiful depiction of the city of Norwich dates to 1558, the year Elizabeth came to the throne (figure 18). It shows a prosperous, well-built town, circled in medieval fashion with a fine wall. Its twin centers, dominating the town, are its cathedral and its castle. But essentially it is an agricultural market town, with fields and flocks both inside and outside its walls. Commerce flows through its numerous gates, and especially along its river, dotted with boats. Technological improvements appear in the form of a mill on the river, the windmills on hills beyond the city, and above all, in the form of the mathematician Cuningham himself, who at bottom center depicts the city in a geometric projection.

If Norwich prospered, then London boomed. In John Norden's 1593 depiction, the cathedral of St. Paul's and the Tower of London are still the largest structures, but grand as they are, they no longer dominate the great metropolis (figure 19). It has spilled beyond its walls into the fields to the north. Across the river to the south runs the dirty sliver of Southwark, home to "The Beare howse" and "The play howse." Across the bottom runs the list of the sights of the city. At upper left are the arms of the queen, but more important, down the sides are the arms of the twelve great guilds that con-

trolled the wealth of the city: the Mercers, Grocers, Drapers, Fishmongers, Goldsmiths, Skinners, Merchant Tailors, Haberdashers, Salters, Ironmongers, Vintners, and Clothworkers.

If the geometry of Norwich connected the town to the country, then London connected England to the world. From it went English ships carrying the products of the countryside and of the city's craftsmen. To it came fine finished goods from the Netherlands and France. Timber came from the Baltic for making furniture. From Germany came exquisite ceramics and silver, often made specifically for the English market. Books came from the international printing centers at Frankfurt, Basel, and Lyon. Trade with Venice brought goods from the Middle East and India (figures 20–21).

Economic development came at a price, of course. It made war more expensive, since war not only killed people and depleted the treasury, it disrupted enterprise and angered everyone who depended on commerce for their livelihoods. It also made England less English. London especially saw the arrival of people from around the world: Africans and Native Americans in small numbers, and refugees from the religious wars in France and the Netherlands in much larger numbers. And it made English culture itself more international. The plays of Marlowe and Shakespeare teem with characters from Italy, France, Germany, Egypt, even Scythia. These cultures were imperfectly understood, to be sure, but they were nonetheless reflected in the great mirror of the stage. The spirit of the emerging

FIGURE 18. "Norwich," from William Cuningham,
The Cosmographical Glasse (London, 1559).
Wing f ZP545 .D27, after p. 8. Newberry Library,
Chicago.

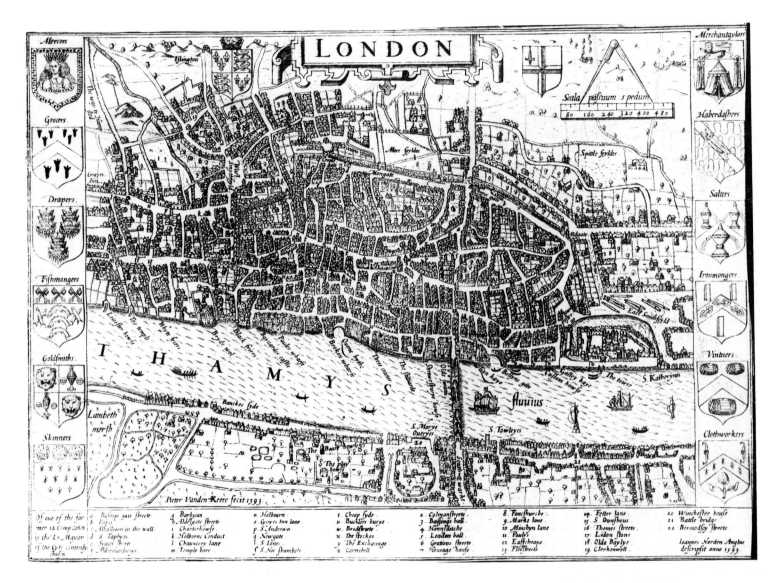

FIGURE 19. "London," from John Norden, *Speculum Britanniae* (London, 1593). Case G45004 .6, after fol. 36. Newberry Library, Chicago.

economy was best summed up by a member of the Muscovy Company, dedicated to opening up trade with far-off Russia: "Traffike is the golden chain concatenation, that ties kingdoms together in mutual amitie: it is the very cement that conjoins the hearts, the hands, yea the souls of nations different in shapes, disagreeing in manners, in speech, in religion, with nerves not to be broken."[1]

NOTE

1. Thomas Smith, *Sir Thomas Smithes Voiage and Entertainment in Rushia* (London, 1605), fol. Br.

FIGURE 20. English merchant, from Cesare Vecellio, *Habiti Antichi, et Moderni di tutto il Mondo* [Ancient and modern costumes of the world] (Venice, 1598). Ayer *335 .V3 1598, p. 277v. Newberry Library, Chicago.

FIGURE 21. Venetian merchant, from Cesare Vecellio, *Habiti Antichi, et Moderni di tutto il Mondo* [Ancient and modern costumes of the world] (Venice, 1598). Ayer *335 .V3 1598, p. 90v. Newberry Library, Chicago.

Elizabeth ruled from Hatfield for a week and then set off for her capital. The steps were carefully staged. First she went to Barnet, just outside the city walls, and stayed with Lord North, who was one of the old councilors dropped from the new lineup but still given honors. She spent most of the following month in London at Somerset House, the palace built by the lord protector with whom she had sparred in the days of her brother, Edward. At last, on December 23, 1558, she moved to the royal palace at Westminster for the Christmas holidays. She still had not been crowned.

Coronation is a sacrament, and Elizabeth needed a secure hold on the church. She used the two months following Mary's death in November 1558 to isolate her major religious opponents and begin installing people who shared her mother's—and her own—Protestant persuasions. At last, on January 14, 1559, Elizabeth was carried in triumph through the streets of London to Westminster Abbey. The big days were carefully planned by the heralds, who handle the arrangements for such historic events. The herald's

How to Survive in Tudor England

The game of survival in Tudor England (1485–1603) was a relatively simple one for thousands of aristocrats and nonaristocrats alike, ones who could remain safely inconspicuous within a radically shifting religious and political climate. But for those who held unshakable convictions and were compelled to assert them, the game was easily lost. In 1535, Sir Thomas More lost his head for not taking Henry VIII's Oath of Allegiance. Anne Askew was burned at the stake in 1544 for Protestant heretical beliefs, while in 1581 the Jesuit Edmund Campion was hanged, drawn, and quartered for treason against Elizabeth. A woman in Essex was hanged in 1577 simply for claiming that Elizabeth was illegitimate and that Mary Queen of Scots should rule in England.

While distinguishing oneself could be a deadly enterprise, some shrewd individuals managed to do so without jeopardizing their lives. Consider Edward North (1496?–1564), who lived and prospered during the reigns of all five Tudor monarchs. Over roughly thirty years, North served in no less than fourteen political offices and other privileged roles, such as managing the vast monastic estates that Henry VIII had confiscated. He was an executor of Henry's will as well as a witness to Edward VI's will. He served as a member of the Privy Council under Henry VIII, Edward, and Mary and was host to Elizabeth's court for nearly a week upon her accession to the throne. Surely, this was a trusted man (figure 22).

Yet how does one inspire trust in a series of rulers, each of whom rewrote the political game plan of his or her predecessor and persecuted formerly loyal subjects? Edward North struck a careful balance by making himself indispensable to the machinery of the monarchy without affiliating himself too closely with the policies of each regime. For example, he witnessed the signing of Edward VI's will (which countermanded Henry's own) and even supported the boy king's chosen successor, Lady Jane Grey. But North had the foresight to avoid putting his signature to the deed of settlement, which disinherited Mary and Elizabeth. Survivors like North must have fashioned themselves in the royal eyes to seem useful but not threatening, self-sufficient and diligent but not too independent, and, above all, compliant to their sovereign's wishes.

North had his close calls. He was suspected of embezzlement by Henry, needed a royal pardon from Mary because of his support of Jane Grey, and was dropped by Elizabeth from the Privy Council. But he succeeded in navigating the perilous waters of Tudor England. He assured his own survival by pleasing the inclinations of his various sovereigns, but also by not pleasing them too much.

—Jonathan Walker

FIGURE 22. Elizabeth I, appointment of Edward North as Lord Lieutenant of Cambridgeshire and the Isle of Ely, May 1, 1559. Kenneth Spencer Research Library, MS J36. University of Kansas, Lawrence.

FIGURE 23. Drawings for the entry into London of Elizabeth I, 1558. MS Egerton 3320, fols. 4v–5r. Reproduced by permission of the British Library.

sketchbook for the royal procession (figure 23) shows trumpeters leading the way, followed by members of the royal household, knights, lords, ambassadors, high officers, and knights and nobles in ascending order, culminating in Thomas Howard, duke of Norfolk and earl marshal of the aristocracy. At last comes Elizabeth riding in a litter, flanked by guards and footmen. Behind her rides Lord Robert Dudley, leading Elizabeth's own horse. Dudley, the son of Lord Protector Northumberland, who had led the Lady Jane Grey conspiracy, was Elizabeth's personal favorite and potential lover. Sandwiched between Norfolk and Dudley, Elizabeth could look forward at the back of her greatest antagonist and principal ally of her dead sister, Mary, and she could look back at the face of her closest supporter: forward at the past, and back at the future. And she could look side to side at the thronging citizens of London who welcomed her rule.

The next morning, January 15, 1559, Elizabeth Tudor sat in Westminster Abbey on the throne of Edward the Confessor, where she was anointed as God's chosen substitute, and received the sword, the ring, the scepter, and the crown that symbolized her position as ruler of England. She was twenty-five years old (figure 24).

The coronation was designed to establish the legitimacy of Elizabeth's reign. In a curious way, the health of the economy depended upon the legitimacy of the ruler. In modern times we are familiar with the idea of consumer confidence: if people are optimistic about the future and about their financial security, they are more likely to buy and sell things, work hard, lend and borrow. Tudor England—and other European nations of the sixteenth century—had a tangible symbol for consumer confidence, in the image of the ruler stamped onto its coins. For all debts were valued, all goods were priced, all wages

FIGURE 24. Elizabeth I, instrument of recovery of the manor of Brantingsten, with Royal Seal, 1579 (detail of obverse). Wing MS +ZW 1.579. Newberry Library, Chicago.

FIGURE 25. Elizabethan sixpence coin, 1581 (obverse). Private collection.

paid, according to their equivalent in precious metals, especially gold and silver. We are used to the idea that paper money is just paper, and coins just little hard pellets, except that they can be exchanged for things, so long as everybody agrees. The Elizabethans needed the reassurance that the coin was worth so much because it really contained that much gold or silver (or even brass). The monarch's face stamped on the coin was the sign that it was really worth something, for the monarch himself or herself was as good as gold (figure 25).

Elizabeth's father and sister had ignored this important fact, though, and had debased the coinage, mixing base metal into the gold and silver, in order to be able to pay their own debts. This not only threatened confidence in the economy, it threatened confidence in the monarch. A person looking at the royal image on a coin might see baseness rather than nobility. Elizabeth understood the crisis in confidence and moved quickly to restore the coinage of the realm.

The crisis in confidence wasn't only about money, however. It was also about gender. Many people opposed on principle the idea of women holding political power, and, before Elizabeth, England had in fact rather poor experiences with women rulers. Mary's reign had ended in failure. Before that, one had to go back to Queen Maud in 1141 to find a woman holding the throne of England in her own right, only to lose it in a civil war. Some queens had wielded great power over their king-husbands, such as Philippa of Hainault (wife of Edward III) and Margaret of Anjou (wife of Henry VI), but they often were viewed with suspicion and resentment, much like an American first lady who dares to take an open role in politics. Think of Lady Macbeth.

Some distinctions may be useful here. A "queen regnant" is one who rules in her own right, like Mary or Elizabeth. A "regent" is one who rules on behalf of the monarch; for instance, Katharine of Aragon was regent when Henry VIII went to war in France in 1513 and did a wonderful job of defending England against the invading king of Scotland. A "consort" is the spouse of a king or queen but does not have any formal power. A "dowager" is the widow of a king and often plays a major role if her child is on the throne.

In fact, the sixteenth century was filled with powerful women who were queens regnant, regents, consorts, and dowagers. There were so many, in fact, that the late sixteenth century saw a backlash among conservative men against women. The most virulent came from John Knox, the leader of the Reformation in Scotland. In *The First Blast of the Trumpet Against the Monstrous Regimen of Women* (first published in 1558), Knox declares: "to promote a woman to bear rule, superiority, dominion or empire above any realm, nation, or city, is repugnant to nature, contumely to God, a thing most contrarious to his revealed will and approved ordinance, and finally it is the subversion of good order, of all equity and justice" (figure 26).[21] Knox argues that, according to natural, civil,

A Century of Queens

Elizabeth of England was the most successful woman ruler of her time, but hardly the only one. Europe in the sixteenth century was crowded with women enthroned or women who ruled on behalf of the kings and emperors in their families.

Although Isabella of Castile died just as the century began, she set the mold. Queen in her own right, she married the king next door (Ferdinand of Aragon) and together they created a unified Spain. She won dramatic victories over the Islamic rulers of southern Spain, financed Columbus, and promulgated her religious faith.

Isabella's daughter Katharine of Aragon was the first wife of Henry VIII. Eight years Henry's senior, Katharine was in many ways his tutor, especially in international affairs (for instance, she showed him how to use code in his diplomatic correspondence). When Henry led an army to France in 1513, Katharine became regent of England and triumphed over an invading Scottish army. When King James IV of Scotland was slain on the battlefield, Katharine sent his bloody shirt to Henry, with compliments.

Henry VIII's other wives had no formal role in government, but some held considerable power behind the scenes. Elizabeth's mother, Anne Boleyn, and Henry's last queen, Catherine Parr, were especially influential in areas of religion. And of course Henry's two daughters, Elizabeth and Mary, sat on the English throne for a total of fifty years.

Across Europe, other women were heads of governments. In the early decades of the century, Margaret of Austria (1480–1530), illegitimate daughter of Emperor Maximilian I, was the Hapsburg regent of the Netherlands from 1507 to 1515, as well as guardian to her nephew Charles, the future Holy Roman Emperor Charles V. From 1559 to 1567, Margaret of Parma (1522–86) occupied the same position in the Netherlands as the Spanish regent. Catherine de Medici (1519–89), daughter of Lorenzo de Medici, duke of Urbino, and widow of Henri II of France (who ruled from 1547 to 1559), became regent in 1560 for her son Charles IX. Mary of Guise (1515–60), queen consort of James V of Scotland, was regent for her daughter Mary Stuart from 1554 to 1559. Mary herself conducted her personal rule of Scotland from 1561, until her flight to England in 1568. The century of Elizabeth was indeed a century of queens.

—Jonathan Walker

PLATE 1. "Nil maius superi vident."
A motet from "Italian Motets and
Madrigals: Henry VIII Part Books,"
circa 1527–28. Case MS VM 1578
M91. Newberry Library, Chicago.

PLATE 2. The Malmsbury-Caird Cup, 1529. Silver-gilt standing cup, height 21.5 cm. Mr. and Mrs. John H. Bryan.

PLATE 3. Royal arms of Queen Elizabeth I, from Robert Cooke, "Armorial bearings of the kings and noble families of Great Britain from the reign of William the Conqueror to that of James I," 1572. Case MS F 0745. 1915. Newberry Library, Chicago.

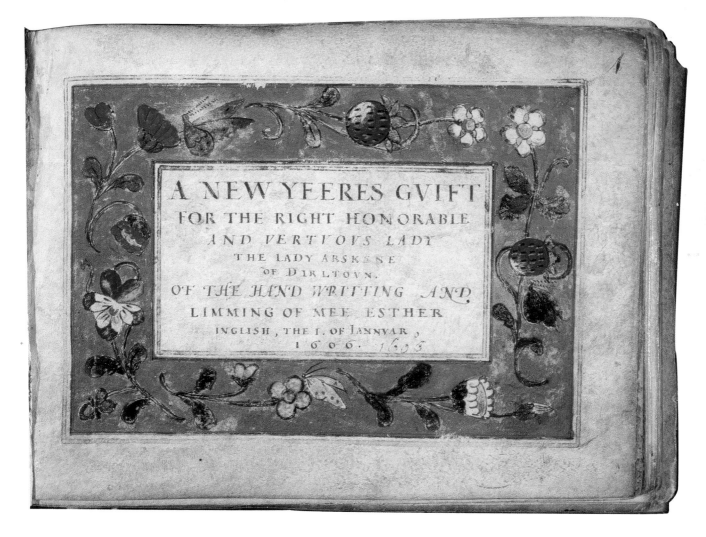

PLATE 4. Title page from Esther Inglish, "A New Yeeres Guift," 1606–7. Wing MS ZW 645 .K29. Newberry Library, Chicago.

PLATE 5. William Scrots (attributed), *Elizabeth I when Princess,* circa 1546–47. Oil on panel, 108.8 × 81.9 cm. The Royal Collection © 2003, Her Majesty Queen Elizabeth II.

OPPOSITE: PLATE 7. Circle of Quentin Massys the Younger, *Sieve Portrait of Queen Elizabeth I,* circa 1580–83. Oil on panel, 112 × 79.5 cm. Mr. and Mrs. John H. Bryan.

PLATE 6. Anonymous, *The Coronation Portrait of Elizabeth I,* circa 1600–1610. Oil on panel, 127.3 × 99.7 cm. Courtesy of the National Portrait Gallery, London.

PLATE 8. Needlework dos-à-dos binding for the Book of Psalms (London, 1628) and the New Testament (London, 1638), circa 1638. Private collection.

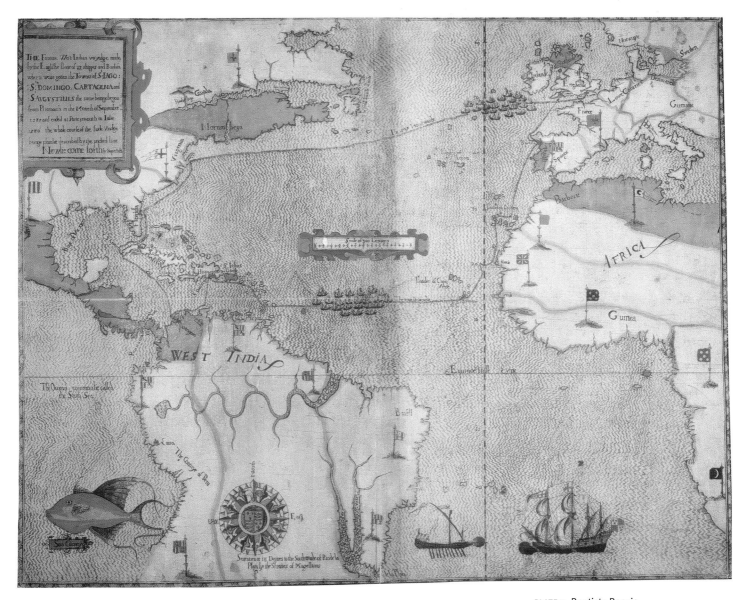

PLATE 9. Baptista Boazio, map of "The famouse West Indian voyadge," 1589. Engraving with color, 41 × 53 cm. Ayer *133 .D7 .B66 1589. Newberry Library, Chicago.

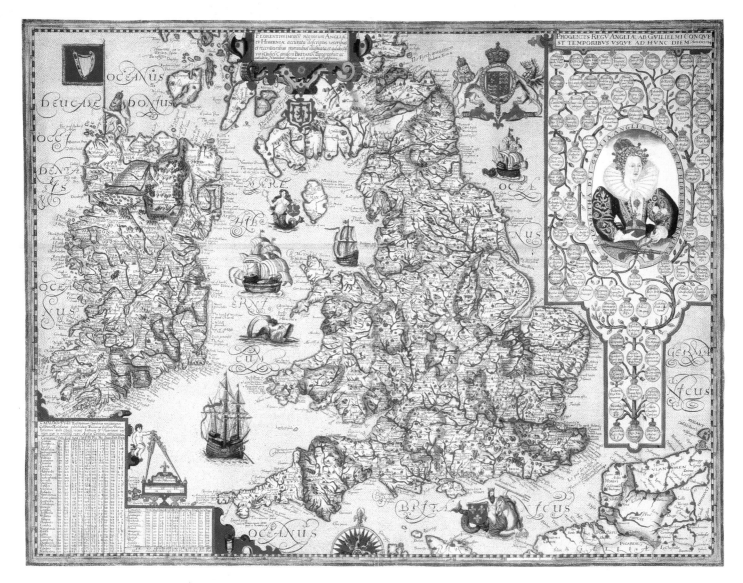

PLATE 10. Anonymous, after Jodocus Hondius, map of England, Wales, and Ireland with genealogy and portrait of Queen Elizabeth I, 1594. Engraving with color, 43 × 58.5 cm. Private collection.

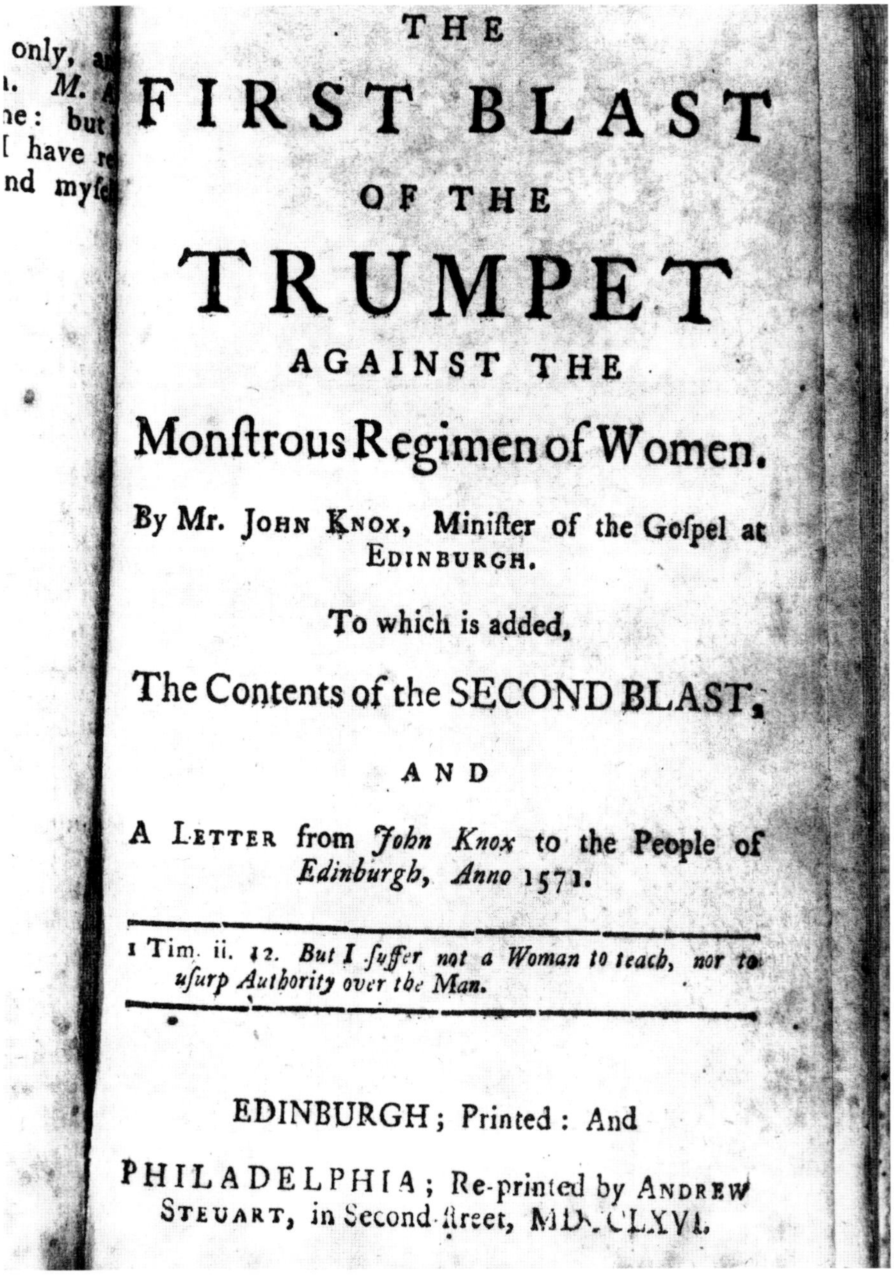

THE

FIRST BLAST

OF THE

TRUMPET

AGAINST THE

Monſtrous Regimen of Women.

By Mr. JOHN KNOX, Miniſter of the Goſpel at EDINBURGH.

To which is added,

The Contents of the SECOND BLAST,

AND

A LETTER from *John Knox* to the People of *Edinburgh*, *Anno* 1571.

1 Tim. ii. 12. *But I ſuffer not a Woman to teach, nor to uſurp Authority over the Man.*

EDINBURGH; Printed: And

PHILADELPHIA; Re-printed by ANDREW STEUART, in Second-ſtreet, MDCCLXVI.

FIGURE 26. Title page from John Knox, *The First Blast of the Trumpet Against the Monstrous Regimen of Women* (Philadelphia, 1766). Case oJN 1239 1766 .B8, no. 2. Newberry Library, Chicago.

and divine laws, "women may and ought to be deposed from authority."[22] This is a revolutionary assertion, aimed at toppling the three Maries who were already Knox's enemies: Mary Queen of Scots; her mother, Mary of Guise, who was regent for her daughter; and Mary Tudor in England.

Knox published his tract anonymously but made little effort to disguise his authorship. Inevitably he offended not only the Catholic queens but also the Protestant Elizabeth, who became monarch just months after the *Blast* was published. One can imagine her reaction to his denunciation of "a woman sitting in judgment, or riding from parliament in the midst of men, having the royal crown upon her head, the sword and scepter borne before her, in sign that the administration of justice was in her power."[23]

John Knox did not speak for all Protestants, and indeed the anti-Catholicism that motivated him also fueled some of the replies that quickly followed. One of the first was written by one of Elizabeth's key supporters. Like Knox, John Aylmer had fled to the Continent when Mary came to power, and he later assisted John Foxe with the Latin version of *Actes and Monuments.* Published only five months after Elizabeth's accession, Aylmer's *An [Harbor] for Faithfull and Trewe Subjectes, agaynst the late blowne blaste, concerninge the Government of Wemen* (1559) praised the new queen as the safe harbor where the English people could find refuge from the lingering national storms of Mary's tyrannous reign. Again like Knox, Aylmer published his book anonymously. But the dedication of the volume to two of Elizabeth's privy councilors suggests that the work was encouraged by the government. Later Aylmer was appointed bishop of London.

But even the defenders could be lukewarm. Aylmer thinks that it is still better to have a man on the throne than a woman, and even the most qualified woman ruler, like Elizabeth, needs to be guided by wise—and male—councilors. In short, he's for women rulers only when God seems to be for them. Another treatise, written by Henry Howard, earl of Northampton, offered scarcely more help. Howard's loyalty to Elizabeth was suspect: his father (the poet Henry Howard, earl of Surrey) and his older brother (the duke of Norfolk) had each been executed for treason, by Henry VIII and Elizabeth, respectively, when Howard set out around 1577 to write his "Dutifull defence of the lawfull regiment of women" (figure 27). He spent thirteen years at the task, during which time he was repeatedly under suspicion of seditious activity related to Mary Queen of Scots, and he was imprisoned in the Tower by Elizabeth more than once.

"A dutifull defence" seems on the surface like a pledge of loyalty to Queen Elizabeth. But Howard's argument on behalf of women is so general that it could apply to any queen, including Mary Queen of Scots, who during this same period was actively conspiring to overthrow Elizabeth and take her place. Later, under Mary Stuart's son

James I, Northampton's divided loyalty at last received its reward when he was appointed in 1603 to the king's Privy Council.

If even the most enlightened men were grudging in their support of women as rulers, some other approach was needed. Elizabeth and those around her found it in the idealization of women that often accompanies their oppression. That is, the argument that women should not be involved in politics was based on two contradictory ideas: that they are incapable of dealing with important matters, and that their delicate and refined natures require that they be protected from the rough-and-tumble world of public af-

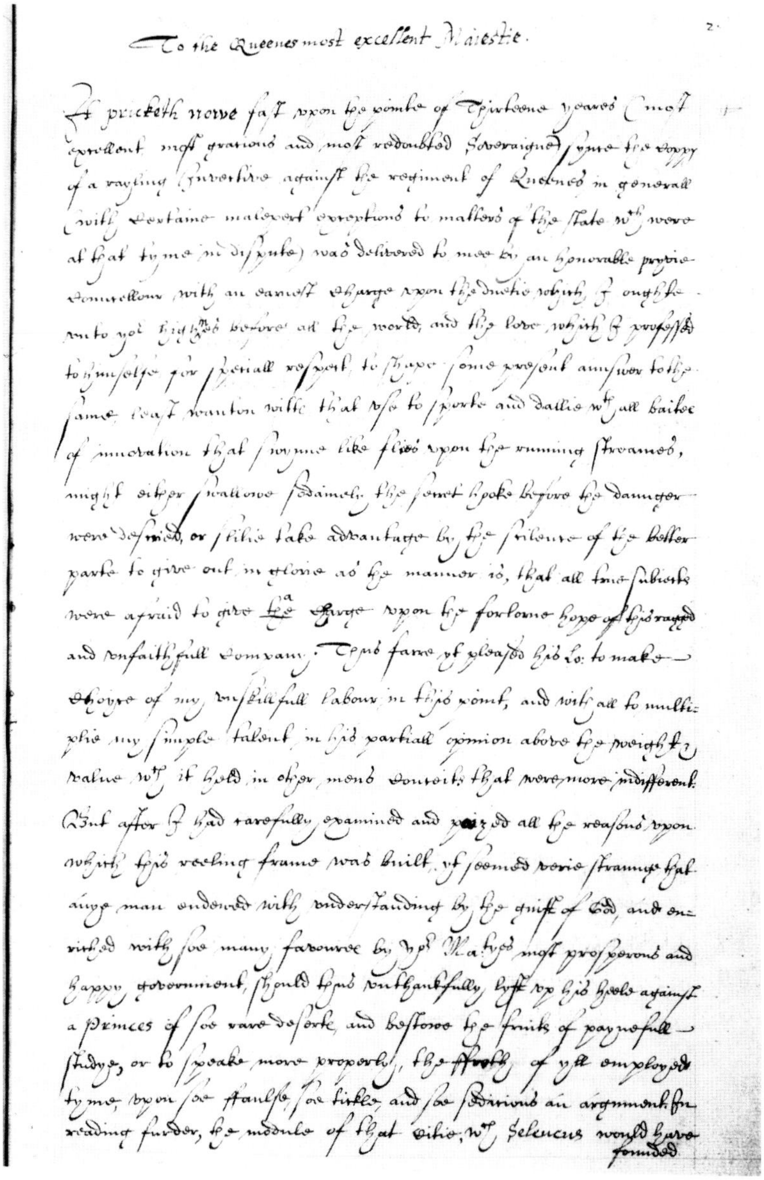
To the Queenes most excellent Maiestie.

FIGURE 27. Dedication to Elizabeth I, from Henry Howard, Earl of Northampton, "A dutifull defence of the lawfull regiment of women," 1589. Case MS fJ 5452 .634, fol. 2r. Newberry Library, Chicago.

PHILOSOPHORVM ΣΟΦΩΤΑΤΩ ÆSCVLAPIO SVO.
Viuere cui vires & robora sana dedisti
Scribere ni vellem, næ robore durior essem.
Ergo mihi (quæ priuato pertingere nulli
CASE datur) tecum satis & satis Astra tueri est.

SPHÆRA CIVITATIS

FIGURE 28. Frontispiece from John Case, *Sphæra Civitatis* [The sphere of state] (Oxford, 1588). Case JO .148. Newberry Library, Chicago.

fairs. The second attitude could be exploited to argue that women—or at least exceptional women—weren't below politics, they were above it. Elizabeth could be portrayed as a transcendent figure who ruled by divine powers, without soiling her hands with the down-and-dirty parts of government.

This tactic would be expressed in many ways, especially in the allegorical portraits of Elizabeth. It found its expression in political theory in John Case's *Sphæra Civitatis* [The sphere of state], published in 1588 (figure 28). Case's book is a commentary on Aristotle's *Politics*, which recommends the monarchy of a perfect ruler as the highest form of government. Although Aristotle thought that men alone could command, and women should obey, Case argued that some women can, through their native intelligence and their experience, become capable rulers. The famous frontispiece depicts Queen Elizabeth standing above a diagram of a Ptolemaic universe, within which the planets correspond to esteemed qualities of a well-ordered state, namely Majesty, Prudence, Fortitude, Religion, Mercy, Eloquence, and Abundance. At the center is "Immovable Justice." As the "head" of government, Elizabeth is positioned like God outside the created order, capably guiding it. At the same time the state is identified with her body. Indeed, Tudor political thought recognized the idea that the monarch actually had two bodies: one natural, which lived and died, and one a mystical "body politic" that was perpetual and encompassed all its subjects. In Case's image of the spheres, the two seem one.

The attack on Elizabeth as a woman is balanced by the idealization of Elizabeth as a woman. This dual myth is so powerful that it has shaped historical accounts of her over four centuries. Often historians give her extra credit, quite reasonably, for overcoming the special obstacles she faced because of her gender, and admire, perhaps unreasonably, the clever devices she developed to exploit it. At other times historians—including the shrewd William Camden—are sucked into the idea that Elizabeth was above the fray, and they describe her as removed from the business of government, which is left to her wise councilors, especially Lord Burghley. At root, though, this is a technique that has less to do with her gender than with the lessons she learned from her father. A clever monarch—like a modern president who is "above politics"—comes out in the open to receive the love and obedience of her subjects, but stays carefully behind the screen of her subordinates when bad things are happening.

Portraits of Elizabeth

In the eighteenth century, the English connoisseur Horace Walpole remarked that it was easy to recognize a portrait of Elizabeth, by the red hair, the distinctive hooked nose, the vast triangular skirt, the huge ruff about the neck, and the explosion of pearls everywhere.

The image is so easy to recognize because it was repeated so often. Less than a dozen artists actually drew or painted her from life. Most used a pattern, borrowed or bought from one of the lucky artists, in order to churn out the finished products— some very good and some extremely bad— for eager buyers. The market lasted throughout her reign and well beyond her

death, and even today her image adorns not only movie posters and book covers but advertisements and candy wrappers.

The most famous portraits are allegorical, showing Elizabeth surrounded by symbols of her personal virtue and her public role. Around 1579, George Gower, who later held the position of Serjeant Painter of England, created an image of Elizabeth holding a sieve (figure 29). This recalls a story from Roman history about a vestal virgin accused of fornication. She carried water from the River Tiber in a sieve, thereby proving that she was chaste. (The theory seems to be that if the sieve didn't leak, then she didn't either.) The painting corresponds in date

---

with Elizabeth's last marriage negotiation, with the duc d'Alençon, and expresses the wishes of most Englishmen that Elizabeth remain the virgin she claimed to be.

Within a few years, a second type of "sieve" portrait appeared, this one from the workshop of a Netherlandish artist named Quentin Massys, a descendent of the great painter of the same name who had known Erasmus, Albrecht Dürer, and Hans Holbein. (As with Gower's Sieve portrait, there are two surviving versions.) Massys the Younger was probably never in England

and was perhaps creating his painting for European court patrons. The figure of Elizabeth now looks left instead of right, and her dress is black instead of red (plate 7). The globe in the background is far more prominent, and in the left background is a column decorated with images of imperial triumph. The painting not only recognizes Elizabeth as a symbol of virtue but also establishes her as a worthy rival to the Hapsburg rulers of Spain and the Holy Roman Empire.

In her later years, Elizabeth's portraits become even more fantastical, as she was de-

picted standing on maps, or even holding rainbows. But in her youth and early years on the throne, the portraits are much more personal. The painting of her at about thirteen (see plate 5) shows a serious, self-controlled young woman. Equally remarkable is a small portrait dating from the first years of Elizabeth's reign (figure 30). Now the serious young woman is dressed all in black, in keeping with the sober manner of dress she adopted during the reigns of her brother and sister. The sobriety is relieved, however, by the elegant line of the dress, the sophisti-

FIGURE 29. George Gower (attributed), *Sieve Portrait of Elizabeth I,* 1579. Oil on panel, 104.1 × 76.2 cm. Folger Shakespeare Library, Washington, D.C.

cated slashing of the sleeves, with satin showing through, and the finely wrought ruffs at neck and wrist. The red hair and the nose mark her as Elizabeth, while the richly brocaded cloth and chair of state behind her mark her as queen.

Remarkable, too, are her hands. Elizabeth's right hand holds a watch, in an elaborate gold case. More puzzling is her left hand, held poised across her lower body with the fingers curled upward. In many portraits of the time, such a hand might hold a glove or touch a jewel or a cross. Here the gesture is unexplained but manages to display the long, elegant fingers of which Elizabeth was always proud.

The space in which she stands is clearly a public one, such as the Presence Chamber of a palace. It opens at the upper left into a vast marble hall or courtyard, lined with magnificent Corinthian columns, with classical statues above them, all suffused with light. The archway in the distance opens onto a sunlit garden or park with trees and a fountain.

While allegorical portraits show Elizabeth standing apart from our world, here she is immersed in it. The watch is the latest luxury good, while the classical architecture is the latest style introduced from Europe to England during the period of her brother, Edward. She is dressed in somber richness and absorbed in thought, a thoroughly modern monarch.

If the later portraits show Elizabeth swathed in her own legend, this early portrait shows an Elizabeth who is ready to create that legend. Her gaze is inward, but behind her is the world of power to which she is about to turn.

FIGURE 30. Anonymous, *Elizabeth I,* circa 1564–67. Oil on panel, 35.6 × 22.9 cm. Mr. and Mrs. John H. Bryan.

RELIGION AND
THE CRISIS OF EUROPE

The problems of religion were far less manageable than the problems of government, even for the most clever and subtle monarch. England, like all of Europe, had been deeply divided since early in the century between Catholic and Protestant—with each group itself divided into contending factions. To make matters worse, the power of religion was entangled with the power of the state. The idea of religious toleration was not widely accepted, and each national ruler expected to enforce a specific religion within his or her borders. Hence differences in belief could quickly become matters of persecution, of civil war, or of war between nations. The inflamed atmosphere is vividly recorded by John Foxe, whose *Actes and Monuments* described the burnings by Mary not only in words, but in simple and powerful woodcuts (figure 31). Answering Foxe with comparable records of Protestant atrocities against Catholics was Richard Verstegan's *Theatrum Crudelitatum Hæreticorum Nostri Temporis* [The theater of cruelty of the heretics in our time] (figure 32).

Elizabeth herself was a living symbol of national religious struggle. Her father had broken with Rome to marry her mother. Her mother had promoted the cause of the Lutherans in England. Her sister had imprisoned her as a threat to the restoration of Catholicism in England. Elizabeth had saved her own life at least in part by conforming—or seeming to conform—to Mary's religious preferences. Once Elizabeth came to the throne, the Protestants who had been suppressed under Mary expected Elizabeth to restore the reformed religion. Many Catholics, who could still remember being suppressed

48

Lord Iefu receiue my foule.

FIGURE 31. The burning of John Hooper, bishop at Gloucester, from John Foxe, *Actes and Monuments* (London, 1583). Case fD78 .308, p. 1510. Newberry Library, Chicago.

FIGURE 32. The persecution of Catholics in Ireland, from Richard Verstegen, *Theatrum Crudelitatum Hæreticorum Nostri Temporis* [The theater of cruelty of the heretics in our time] (Antwerp, 1592). Case D78 .938, p. 81. Newberry Library, Chicago.

under Edward, simply expected the worst. Foxe, as we have seen, proclaimed that Elizabeth had been preserved by God for the salvation of the true faith. The Geneva Bible, prepared from their place of exile in Switzerland by those who had fled Mary, carried an epistle "To The Most Vertuous and Noble Quene Elisabet, Quene of England" (figure 33).

Only a few voices dared call for moderation, in the tradition of Erasmus, who had attempted to dampen the early flames of reformation by appealing for dialogue and internal reform. The Portuguese Catholic scholar Jeronymo da Fonseca Osorio, a follower of Erasmus, addressed a treatise to the new English queen entitled *A Pearle for a Prynce.* Osorio argues that "a woman wisely ruling is more to be marveled at than a man."[24] He then tries to convince Elizabeth that she should embrace Catholicism, otherwise she will be consumed by the fires of religious conflict. "Blessed are the peacemakers," says the Gospel, but too often the peacemakers simply incur the wrath of those on both extremes. Osorio died at the hands of the Inquisition for his reformist beliefs. Even more ironically, Osorio's house was burned by English troops when Robert Devereux, the earl of Essex, raided the Spanish coast in 1596, and the books in his library were carted away, ending up in the Bodleian Library at Oxford.

As queen, Elizabeth proved to be her mother's daughter. She appointed bishops who were inclined to the cause of reform and who opposed the power of Rome. She re-established the English mass and the English Bible. The frontispiece to the new Bible shows Elizabeth as a young ruler, her hair flowing to mark her unmarried status (figure 34). She holds the orb and scepter, and is surrounded by the heraldic signs of her royal house, all set in a stylish Italian design. At the bottom is a verse from Romans 1:16: "For I am not ashamed of the Gospel of Christ, because it is the power of God unto salvation to all that believe."[25] Ironically the verse is in Latin—though it is the English Bible that Elizabeth here embraces.

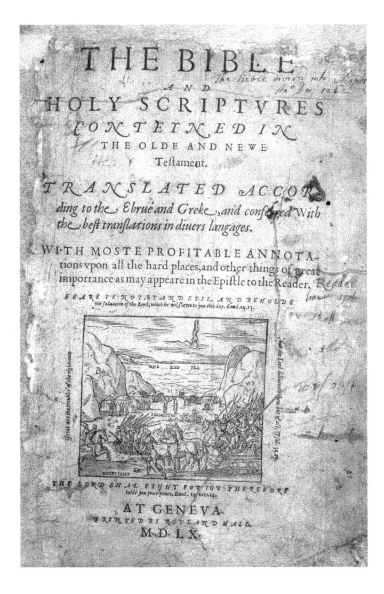

FIGURE 33. Title page from *The Bible and Holy Scriptures Conteyned in the Olde and Newe Testament* ["Geneva Bible"] (Geneva, 1560). Case C22 .560. Newberry Library, Chicago.

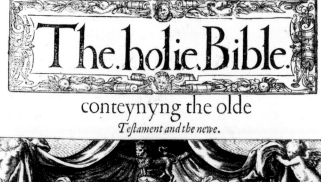

New rules for churches were established that restored many of the reformation practices of Edward's period. Images and shrines were forbidden in churches, in observance of the commandment against the worship of idols. Sermons were required, and the church service was changed back to English from Latin (figure 35).

In all this, Elizabeth was also her father's daughter, since her actions asserted royal authority over the state religion and established her own role as governor of the church. Foxe recognized this in *Actes and Monuments* in a beautiful woodcut showing her enthroned within the capital letter "C," like the emperor Constantine, who gave protection to Christianity after a period of persecution (figure 36).[26]

ARTICLES.

Ⓕⓘⓡⓢⓣ, whether any Parſon, Ѡⓘⓒⓐⓡ, oʒ Curate, be reſidẽt continually vpon his Benefice, doⸯyng his duetie in preachyng, redyng and duelye miniⸯſtryng the holye Sacramentes.   Reſidence. 1

Item, whether in their Churches Falſe miraⸯ 2 and Chappelles, all Images, Shʒynes, all Tables, Candelſtickes, Trindelles, oʒ rolles of war, pictures, payntynges, and all other monumentes of fayned and falſe miracles, pylgrymages, Idolatrye, and ſuperſtition, be remoued, abolyⸯſhed, and deſtroyed.

Item, whether they do not euery Holydaye 3 when they haue no Sermon, immediatly after Loʒdes the Goſpell, openly, playnely, and diſtinctly, reⸯ prayer. ſyte to theyʒ paryſhioners in the Pulpitte, the Loʒdes prayer, the beliefe, and the tenne Commaundementes in Englyſhe.

Item, whether they do charge fathers and 4 mothers, maiſters, and gouernours of youth, to To bʒyng bʒyng them vp in ſome vertuous ſtudye and ocⸯ vp youth. cupation.

A ii   Item,

FIGURE 35. Church of England, *Articles to be enquired in the visitation, in the firste yere of the raigne of our moste dread Soveraigne Lady, Elizabeth by the grace of God, of Englande, Fraunce, and Irelande, Queene, defendour of the faith* (London, 1559). Wing ZP 545 .J93, fol. A2r. Newberry Library, Chicago.

FIGURE 36. Decorative capital "C," from John Foxe, *Actes and Monuments* (London, 1583). Case fD78 .308, fol. §5r. Newberry Library, Chicago.

Elizabeth's personal religious beliefs are hard to know, since she herself didn't talk about them much, and the descriptions offered by those around her are designed to suit their own purposes. Clearly she was Protestant—she could hardly be anything else—but she never protested quite enough for the extreme reformers. They were greatly irritated that she kept a crucifix in her private chapel, and three times during her reign persons broke in and vandalized it.

First and foremost Elizabeth belonged to the religion of monarchy. Whenever Protestantism threatened to infringe on royal authority, she seemed to be against it. She didn't like being lectured by preachers about what her duty was. Above all, she didn't like religious agitation and conflict, since they might lead to civil strife and even civil war. All this came to a head when her own archbishop of Canterbury, Edmund Grindal, stirred up religious debate and then dared to proclaim to her, "Remember, Madam, that you are

ELIZABETH I

a mortal creature. . . . Is it not a corruptible body, which must return to his earth again, God know how soon? . . . And although you are a mighty prince, yet remember that He which dwelleth in heaven is mightier."[27] Grindal ended up under house arrest, with his powers placed in the hands of others.

The dynastic implications of Elizabeth's religious stance are illustrated by a strange and remarkable painting in the Art Institute of Chicago (figure 37). Executed in 1597, the painting is a composite portrait of Henry VIII, Edward VI, and Elizabeth, each represented at the age when he or she sat on the throne. Across the top is written the startling caption, "Professors and Defendors of the True Catholicke Faythe." The title "Defender of the Faith," given to Henry VIII in 1521 by Pope Leo X as a reward for Henry's treatise against Luther, is here passed on to his two younger children. The one genuinely and consistently Catholic Tudor monarch, Mary, is simply left out of the inheritance. Instead, the reformed English church is described as "Catholic," meaning "universal"—or at least universal within the boundaries of England. By implication, the English church claims to be the true heir to the church of the apostles, and the church supervised by the bishop of Rome (as the pope was called by Protestants) is to mind its own business. Above all, the painting suggests that true Christianity is to be found in the person of the ruler.

Under Elizabeth's greatest archbishop, Matthew Parker, the English state church created for itself a history tracing back to the church of Christ's apostles and the early English church of the Anglo-Saxons. It also developed a theology of its own, especially in the work of Richard Hooker, that established it as a sensible middle course, aligned with divine will and human nature, and not just an awkward compromise dictated by the political expedience of the ruler. Only these steps allowed the state church of England to become an Anglican Church that could hope to hold the hearts and minds of its people.

Since questions of religion in the sixteenth century were dynastic as well as devotional, they inevitably involved not only domestic policy but also international relations. England's great international rival in the middle ages was France (figure 38). A French duke, William of Normandy, had conquered England in 1066, and throughout the fourteenth and early fifteenth centuries, England had tried to return the favor by conquering France. One reason Mary Tudor was so unpopular was that she lost England's last French possessions, even though she, and Elizabeth after her, continued to claim the title of queen of France.

If England's natural enemy was France, its natural allies were the regions bordering France, namely Spain and the Netherlands. Trade with the Netherlands was always central to the economy of England. Spain was the center of dynastic alliances, from the marriage of John of Gaunt in 1372 to Constance of Castile, to the marriage of Henry VIII

FIGURE 37. British School, *Henry VIII, Edward VI, and Elizabeth I* ["Professors and Defendors of the True Catholicke Faythe"], 1597. Oil on panel, 63 × 78 cm. Gift of Kate S. Buckingham, Art Institute of Chicago.

56

FIGURE 38. "Paris," from Georg Braun and Franz Hogenberg, *Civitatis Orbis Terrarum* [Cities of the world] (Cologne, 1577). Ayer *135 B8 .1573, vol. 1, plate 7. Newberry Library, Chicago.

in 1509 to Katharine of Aragon, the daughter of the celebrated Ferdinand of Aragon and Isabella of Castile.

Henry's divorce and the reformation in England turned all this on its head. Charles V, Holy Roman Emperor, king of Spain, and nephew to Katharine of Aragon, held such power over the papacy that he could block Henry's divorce, leaving Henry no option except to break with Rome if he was to marry Elizabeth's mother. Mary Tudor was simply returning to the normal state of affairs when she married Charles's son and heir, Philip II, and formed an alliance with Spain against France. After Mary's death, Philip contemplated marriage to Elizabeth, as improbable as this seems in light of later events. At the very least, he wanted to keep Mary Queen of Scots off the throne, since she was dowager queen of France and would presumably have brought England into alliance with France. But once Elizabeth was secure on the throne, neither she nor Philip seems to have seen much logic in the alliance. In the "Queen Mary Atlas," the arms of Spain, quartered with those of England, were scratched out—legend says by Elizabeth herself (figure 39). Gradually, England and Spain moved toward conflict, especially over the Spanish Netherlands, which was itself divided between Protestants and Catholics. As Philip moved to restore the supremacy of Catholicism, Dutch Protestants turned to their near neighbor England for financial and military support.

France meanwhile descended into a religious civil war of its own, which flared hot and cold throughout the second half of the century. The massacre of French Protestants (Huguenots) in Paris on August 24, 1572, inflamed English public opinion. Increasing numbers of Protestant refugees from both France and the Netherlands arrived in En-

FIGURE 39. Royal arms of England and Spain. Detail of "Occidens," from Diego Homem, "Queen Mary Atlas," 1558. MS Additional 5415A, fol. 10r. Reproduced by permission of the British Library.

gland. For Elizabeth, religious war posed a triple danger. She could be drawn into the internal struggles of any number of nations. She could be forced to ally with France against Spain or with Spain against France. Or worst of all, she could find herself facing either or both of the Catholic superpowers, France and Spain, with only the weak forces of Dutch or German Protestants to help her.

Elizabeth's foreign policy in many ways matched her domestic policy. At home she would favor Protestants, up to a limit, but work to keep English Catholics loyal to the crown, even as she forbade their religious practices. Internationally, she would support Protestants in their resistance to the Catholic governments of France and Spain, while trying to avoid provoking either—and especially Spain—into all-out war. One tactic was to minimize the differences among Christians, and to emphasize what she saw as deeper and more lasting differences between Christians and others, especially Muslims. Hence in 1565, the Spanish ambassador, Guzman de Silva, quoted her in his dispatches as saying that "many people think we [English Protestants] are Turks or Moors here, whereas we only differ from other Catholics in things of small importance."[28]

At a time when Protestants and Catholics were calling each other heretics, Elizabeth is not so subtly suggesting that the "real" heretics, from a European Christian point of view, were the "Turks or Moors." At the same time she is suggesting that if Philip II wants to fight somebody, he should forget about the Protestants to the north and west and turn around to confront the Muslim powers to the south and east. Indeed (as readers of Shakespeare's *Othello* know) the Christian states of Europe, especially in Spain and Italy, were locked in a centuries-long struggle with the Islamic powers of North Africa and the eastern Mediterranean. It was Ferdinand and Isabella—the grandparents of Mary Tudor and great-grandparents of Philip II—who had driven the last Muslim armies out of Spain in 1492. Philip himself waged a savage civil war in the 1560s against the Muslim population of Spain. And in 1571, Philip and his Italian allies won a huge naval victory over Salim II of Turkey to gain control of the Mediterranean. This is the sixteenth-century phase of the "clash of civilizations" whose long shadow still lies sadly over us all.[29]

Elizabeth nearly succeeded in her policy of avoiding conflict both at home and abroad, or deflecting it from herself when it was unavoidable. But as the European atmosphere worsened, some in England and abroad hoped that the death of Elizabeth would open a path to the throne for the Catholic Mary Queen of Scots. So in 1570, Pope Pius V denounced "that servant of all iniquity, Elizabeth, pretended Queen of England, with whom, as in a most secure place, all the worst kind of men find a refuge." He declared that "the aforesaid Elizabeth is a heretic and a favourer of heretics . . . and that she is wholly deprived of her pretended right to the aforesaid kingdom."[30] The papal bull was a document that served both extremes. For those who opposed Elizabeth to the death, it was an open call for her assassination. For those who most virulently supported her, it was an open call for preemptive action or reprisal against her enemies. It would play this double role for over a century in English political life, and would be reprinted in order to inflame public opinion in the time of England's last Catholic monarch, James II.

In many ways, Elizabeth's attitudes and actions toward religion strengthened the role of private religious devotion. If social order was to be maintained through religious calm, then the theater for displaying strong religious feeling moved inside to the realm of conscience. Elizabeth herself enacted this idea for her people by expressing a preference for private over public worship. "She many times said . . . that she had rather talk with God devoutly by prayer, than hear others speak eloquently of God," reports William Camden on Elizabeth.[31] Most famously, Sir Francis Bacon wrote about Elizabeth's "not liking to make windows into men's hearts and secret thoughts."[32] (This sounds at first like a call for religious tolerance, but it was easier on those Protestants who practiced outside the Anglican Church than it was on Catholics, whose doctrine required the celebration of the mass.)

Elizabethan books reflect the dichotomy between public and private devotion. *The Booke of Common prayer* was grand in size and meant to be kept in each parish church for use and reference as a testament to the state religion (figure 40). The final page notes that it is printed by royal command. The device shows a pelican piercing its own breast to feed its children with its blood. This is an allegorical reference to Christ, who shed his blood for his followers, but it was also a device used by Elizabeth herself. The mottos around the image and the flanking figures of Prudence and Justice reinforce the identification of law, monarch, and religion. In contrast, a beautiful little book from the first half of the seventeenth century combines the New Testament with the hymnal (plate 8). It is the sort of personal book that the princess Elizabeth carried in her youthful portrait (see plate 5). Its cover is beautifully embroidered with delicate flowers, and worn through careful use.

The character of Elizabethan private devotion can also be glimpsed in a humble but elegant brass candlestick of the period (figure 41). On its base is engraved an enigmatic proverb: "The halte and blind ever ben be hynd."[33] This seems to allude to Luke 14:16–24, where Christ tells a parable about a rich man who invites guests to his feast, but they are too busy to come. So he sends his servants to bring in the lame and blind from the streets to enjoy the feast. His point is that the high and mighty of the earth are not likely to hear God's call, but the low and humble will.

But what does this have to do with the candlestick, which seems to have only bad news for the lame and blind? The candlestick offers a challenge and a promise. When you pick up the candlestick, you are standing behind it, and without its light, you are in

Imprinted at London, by Richarde Iugge, Printer to the Queenes Maieſtie.

Cum priuilegio Regiæ Maieſtatis.

PRO LEGE REGE ET GREGE

LOVE KEPITH THE LAWE OBEYETH THE KYNGE, AND IS GOOD TO THE COMMEN WELTHE

PRVDENCIA   IVSTICIA

FIGURE 40. Colophon from *The Booke of Common prayer* (London, 1577). Case C8726 .577, fol. N4v. Newberry Library, Chicago.

FIGURE 41. Brass candlestick, circa 1500–1550, 17.5 × 11.4 cm. Mr. and Mrs. John H. Bryan.

darkness and likely to stumble. But follow the light, and you will see and walk. For many Elizabethans, of all religious callings, the true way was to shut out the din of religious strife and in simple, everyday acts involving simple, everyday objects, meditate on the actions of the spirit.

Elizabeth's own preference for private devotion was proclaimed widely by an often-reprinted book entitled *A booke of christian prayers* but known popularly as "The Queen's Prayerbook" (figure 42). The content of the volume changes over its many editions, but all have an assortment of prayers, including some for the health and safety of the queen and some composed by the queen herself. The beautiful frontispiece shows Elizabeth kneeling in prayer, her scepter and sword of state set aside. On the lectern in front of her is open a book of devotion—perhaps this very book. But she does not need to read the words, for her face is turned upward toward God as she recites the words in

FIGURE 42. Frontispiece from Richard Day, *A booke of christian prayers* ["The Queen's Prayerbook"] (London, 1581). 248 D33b 1581. Courtesy of the Rare Book and Special Collections Library, University of Illinois at Urbana-Champaign.

her heart. All this takes place in the secrecy of an inner room, recessed from the lighted, public space that we glimpse through a parted curtain. Hence she enacts Matthew 6:5–6: "And when thou prayest, thou shalt not be as the hypocrites are. For they love to stand, praying in the synagogues and in the corners of the streets, that they may be seen of men. Verily I say unto you, they have their reward. But when thou prayest, enter into thy chamber, and when thou hast shut thy door, pray to thy father, which is in secret, and thy father which seeth in secret shall reward thee openly."[34]

The irony here of course is that the "Queen's Prayerbook" is promising that it will let us see into the secret of the queen's prayers. At the very back of the picture, barely visible through the parted curtain, are two windows. Elizabeth, according to Bacon, did not like to make windows into men's hearts. But in order to lead her nation through the morass of religious conflict, she had to allow men to believe that they had a window into her own.

MARRIAGE AND
VIRGINITY

Elizabeth was essentially unchallenged when she came to the throne and had remarkable success in establishing her rule. But hanging over it always was the question of whether—and whom—she would marry. The question was a double one, posed by those who did not believe that a woman could rule by herself, and posed by all who wanted to know who would come after her.

We now know that Elizabeth would never marry, but historians debate whether she ever planned to. As a princess, she had known that she was likely to end up married to whomever her brother or her sister or the lord protector or the Privy Council picked for her. As queen she had much more control over the matter, but she still knew that her choice had to be popular with the nation. After all, her sister's marriage to Philip II of Spain had been a political disaster. So in her first speech to Parliament in 1559, it was the only subject she talked about.

Elizabeth's speech exists in several versions, all of which are recollections written down by people who were there and heard what she said—or rather, what Lord Keeper Nicholas Bacon (the father of Sir Francis Bacon) said on her behalf. The most reliable version ends with a famous declaration that "in the end, this shall be for me sufficient: that a marble stone shall declare that a queen, having reigned such a time, lived and died a virgin." This sounds like she has made up her mind not to marry, but in the rest of the speech she explores the logical alternatives. As a princess, she might have married out of either ambition or fear. Now that she is queen, all that has changed, and she is perfectly content to remain unmarried, if that is what is best for the country. If she does marry, it will be to someone who will be "as careful for the preservation of the realm and you as myself." Besides, even if she had a child, that person might not be a good ruler. In sum, she knows that Parliament wants her to marry and have a child to inherit the throne. She shares their concern, but assures them that, even if she doesn't marry, things will turn out all right. Above all, she politely tells them that she and God alone will make the decision.[35]

Elizabeth had a fair number of prospects. In addition to Philip of Spain she could choose from King Eric of Sweden, Archduke Charles of Austria, and several French princes, plus an ample store of handsome and ambitious English noblemen, including her personal favorite, Robert Dudley, earl of Leicester (figure 43). Foreign princes meant foreign alliances, though, which neither Elizabeth nor the English much cared for. And if she married an Englishman, he would be put up above all the other Englishmen, and so each was against her marrying any of the others. Dudley, who had the best chance, had

FIGURE 43. Nicholas Hilliard, *Robert Dudley, Earl of Leicester,* 1576. Ink and color on card, diameter 4.5 cm. Courtesy of the National Portrait Gallery, London.

ELIZABETH I

made the mistake of already being married, and then his wife made the mistake of falling down the steps and killing herself. So Dudley's chances didn't look too good either.

In 1562 Elizabeth fell sick with smallpox and barely recovered. The Parliament of 1563 returned to the subject of marriage impatiently, first in January and then again in April. In January, she delayed, telling the members that so great a matter required careful thought (as if she hadn't been thinking about it for four years already). Then she reminded them, in flavorful language, how much they owed her already, simply because she had survived to occupy the throne. "I trust you likewise do not forget that by me you were delivered whilst you were hanging on the bough ready to fall into the mud—yea, to be drowned in the dung."[36]

Parliament gave her ten weeks and then petitioned again, this time asking her "to dispose yourself to marry where it shall please you, with whom it shall please you, and as soon as it shall please you."[37] At the same time, they asked her to name a successor in case she died without a child. Elizabeth's answer was short but carefully worded. She herself worked on the draft, scribbling corrections and insertions (figure 44). Bacon delivered it on April 10, 1563. Some (he said on her behalf) believed that she was determined never to marry. "Pull out that heresy, for your belief is there awry." An unmarried life may be best for a "private woman"—that is, a common citizen—but not for a ruler. "And if I can bend my liking to your need I will not resist such a mind."[38] This was the closest Elizabeth had come so far to a public declaration that she would marry.

In 1566 Parliament reassembled and they went at it again. In December, Elizabeth spoke to the members—now for the fourth time—about marriage: "And therefore I say again I will marry as soon as I can conveniently . . . And I hope to have children; otherwise I would never marry."[39] And she lashed at them for suggesting that she was careless about the matter, or didn't care about England.

But Parliament persisted, and as it pressed on, she dug in. She tried to forbid the members even to talk about marriage or succession, but that backfired, because it turned into a free speech issue. There was, to be sure, not a great deal of free speech in sixteenth-century England, but Parliament was one place where it was assured, and Parliament was going to defend that right as vehemently as the queen was going to defend her right to choose. By early January 1567, toward the end of the twelve-day Christmas season, they were at a stand-off. Again Elizabeth carefully drafted her reply—or "admonition," as she called it—working and reworking the words that Bacon would deliver for her (figure 45). In the draft, she denounces the "lip-labored orations" of their "lewd endeavor" and calls the members "wholly ignorant" and "simple."[40] That's the nice part. Then she breaks them into four categories: first, those who didn't realize what they were getting into;

FIGURE 44. Elizabeth I, answer to the Lords' petition that she marry, April 10, 1563. MS Lansdowne 94, art. 15B, fol. 30r. Reproduced by permission of the British Library.

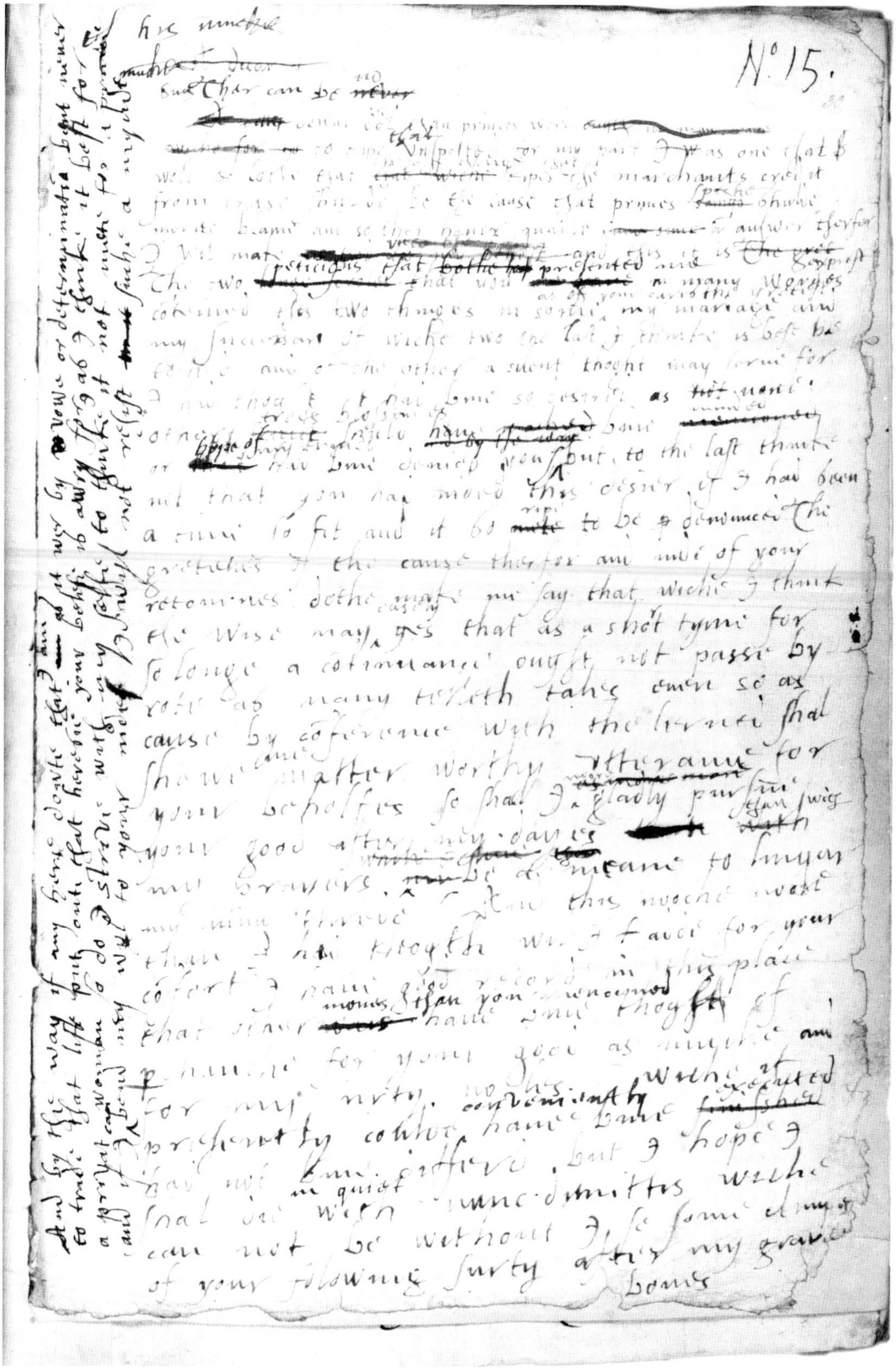

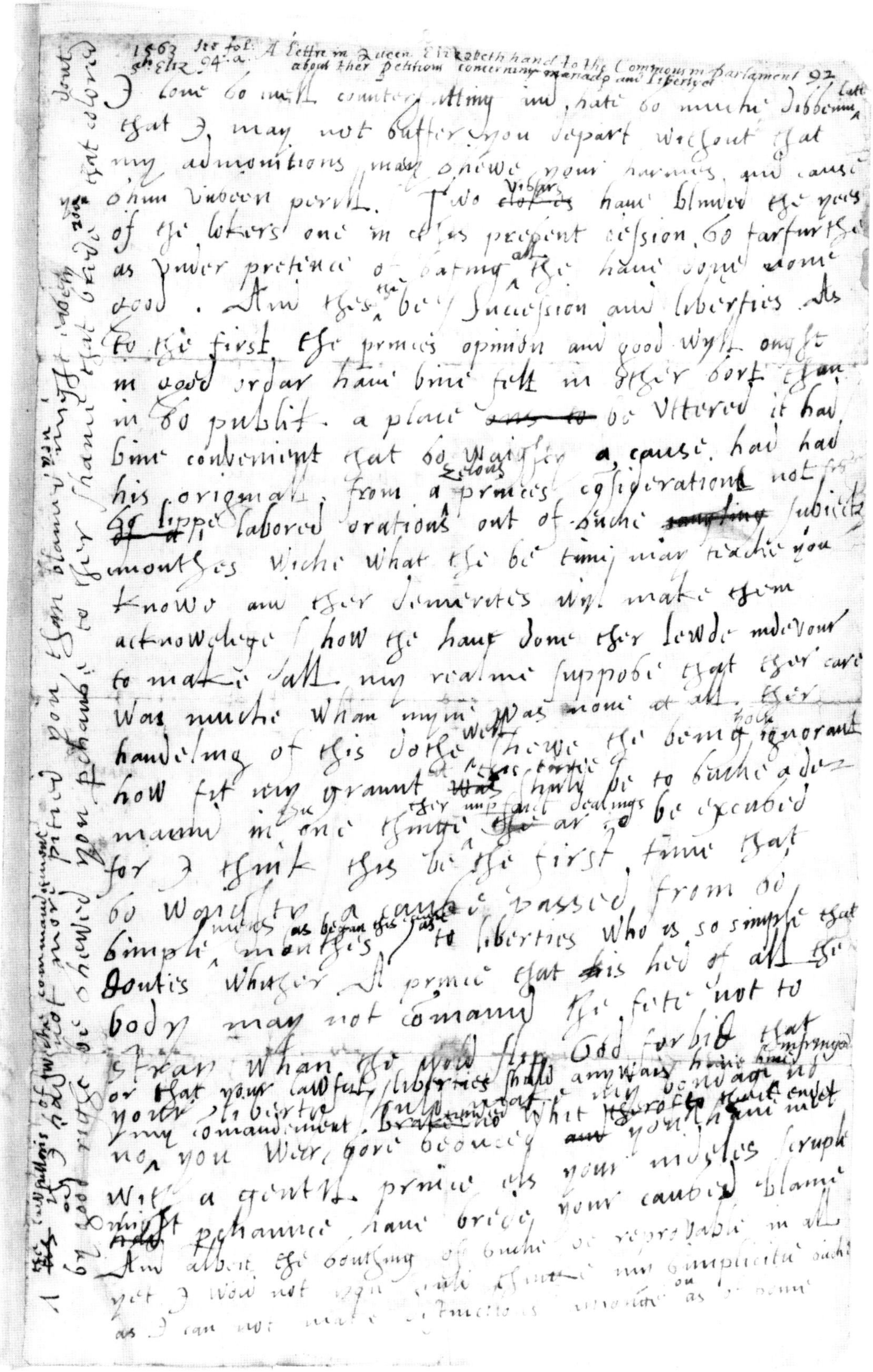

FIGURE 45. Elizabeth I, speech dissolving Parliament, January 2, 1567, version 1. MS Cotton Charter IV.38 (2). Reproduced by permission of the British Library.

second, those who didn't understand the situation; third, those who understood but followed the lead of others; and finally, the instigators themselves.

This would have been stern stuff from the daughter of Henry VIII. But when the moment came, Bacon did not recite what Elizabeth had written. Instead, he made an initial reply, and then the queen herself rose dramatically and added "a few words further." We have only reports of what she said, written down immediately afterward by those who were there. But we may believe that they are accurate, since, as Elizabeth remarked, "princes' own words be better printed in the hearers' memory than those spoken by her commandment." The polite accusations of the draft now become direct and vivid, as she names the groups who engineered the confrontation: "the broachers," "the speakers," "the agreers," and "those which sat still mute and meddled not therewith, but rather wondered."[41] Only the last are wholly excused. The rest are guilty of dissimulation and mischief, and some among them, she declares, are her enemies. The tongue-lashing completed, she wished them a merry Christmas, and Parliament was dissolved.

In the end, Parliament won the battle over free speech, and Elizabeth won the battle over the marriage. She had said she would marry when it was convenient, but it never seemed to be. The foreign princes one by one were found to be

The Voice of the Queen

Queen Elizabeth was a prolific author. Poems, prayers, letters, and speeches by the hundreds survive in her hand, or in early copies and reports. Yet it is often difficult to know exactly what she wrote or said.

There are good reasons for this. Before becoming queen, Elizabeth was in constant danger, and the slightest misstatement or indiscreet sentence could be fatal. She learned to speak and write in guarded, indirect ways, communicating by suggestion rather than plain language.

As queen, she knew that she spoke not just for herself, but for her government and for the nation. And like any skillful ruler, she worked with a talented staff, including William Cecil, his son Robert Cecil, Sir Nicholas Bacon, and others. Sometimes they prepared a draft of a speech for her to edit. Occasionally she sketched the first draft herself and then they polished it. Often, after she delivered a speech, they or she—or both—would go back and create an improved version to be published.

Quickly the members of this "Elizabeth committee" learned to write for their mistress's voice, and an "Elizabeth style" emerged. It is at times maddeningly circuitous, at times shockingly direct and earthy, depending on whether she wanted to hide her real intentions or be clearly understood. This may or may not be exactly the voice of Elizabeth Tudor, but it is certainly the voice of the queen. Since the monarch did not

usually deliver his or her own speeches, but relied on the lord chancellor to do it, this blending of "personal" and "official" voices is critical to their effect. Elizabeth's speeches to Parliament were often reprinted, and in the seventeenth century were collected by Simonds D'Ewes. (The frontispiece to the 1693 edition of his work has updated the clothing style, but Elizabeth herself is still recognizable, as are Burghley and Sir Francis Walsingham, Burghley's successor as secretary of state, behind her) (figure 46).

In her poems and prayers, Elizabeth works her style to a different effect. Her prayers ask protection for the English people and for herself as their guardian. In doing so, they probe her motives and her actions to ensure that they can withstand divine scrutiny. In effect, Elizabeth gives voice to the conscience of a nation. In her poems, she frequently achieves a more "personal" voice not by saying anything especially revealing, but by saying that she would speak her private thoughts, if only her position allowed it. The poems hint at the complexity of the thoughts and emotions that lie behind the mask of power.

FIGURE 46. Frontispiece from Simonds D'Ewes, *A Compleat Journal of the Votes, Speeches and Debates, both of the House of Lords and House of Commons Throughout the whole Reign of Queen Elizabeth, Of Glorious Memory* (London, 1693). Case fK 1454 .231. Newberry Library, Chicago.

too old or too young or too stupid or ugly or just plain too foreign. The English candidates faced intense opposition from one another: they were like a firing squad drawn up in a circle. If Elizabeth had married to please herself, she would certainly have chosen the earl of Leicester. But when his wife turned up dead at the bottom of the stairs—did she fall or was she pushed?—the scandalmongers moved in. Leicester became the object of scurrilous pamphlets both in England and abroad, accusing him not only of adultery and murder but of an actual alliance with Satan. Leicester served Elizabeth loyally until his death in 1588, but the scandal never entirely went away. The slanders simply circulated under the new title of "The Earle of Leicesters Ghoste" (figure 47), and told how the earl's shade rose from the grave to confess his sins.

As late as the mid-1570s, Leicester may still have dreamed of marrying Elizabeth,

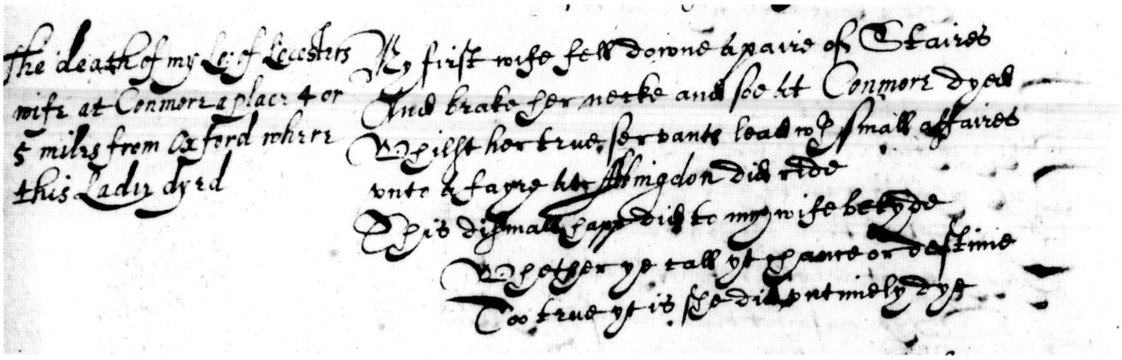
The death of my Lo: of Leicesters wife at Conmore a place 4 or 5 miles from Oxford where this Ladie dyed

My first wife fell downe a paire of staires
And brake her necke and so at Conmore dyed
Whilst her true servants lead my small affaires
unto a fayre at Abingdon did ride

FIGURE 47. The death of Amy Robsart, first wife of Robert Dudley, from Thomas Rogers, "The Earle of Leicesters Ghoste," circa 1602–4. Case MS Y185 .L53. Newberry Library, Chicago.

The Progress of 1575

Throughout the year, Elizabeth would move about among her castles and palaces in and around London: Whitehall Palace, Greenwich, Hampton Court, and Windsor. But in the summer, London was hot, smelly, and disease-ridden, and Elizabeth liked to escape to the countryside. Her "progresses," or summer trips, were also designed so that she could see and be seen by her people. She journeyed from county to county, sometimes staying at her own country houses and lodges, but more often visiting the homes of her chief counselors and nobility.

The queen did not travel light. Clothing and furniture went with her, plus a huge retinue of courtiers, officials, servants, retainers, and hangers-on, and all their stuff as well. Four hundred to six hundred carts might be required, stretching for miles along the road. Elizabeth moved slowly across the landscape, and the way would be lined with her subjects hoping to glimpse the monarch or hear her speak (figure 48).

The most fabulous excursion was the progress of 1575, which lasted from late May into early September. Each town and each nobleman along the route prepared for the royal visit. At Leicester, taxes were levied to

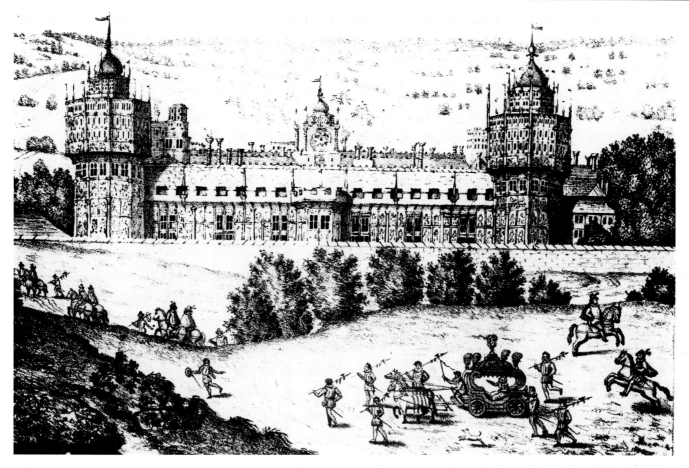

buy red-and-scarlet gowns for the mayor and council members, but then the queen chose another route and didn't come. At Lichfield, the streets were cleared of unsavory sights and persons. One person was paid a shilling to take down the scaffold, and another was paid five shillings to keep "mad Richard" out of the way when the queen was in town. Most significant, perhaps, was a payment of over eight shillings to a group of actors, who included James Burbage, the father of Shakespeare's colleague Richard Burbage.

At Worcester, the preparations were even more thorough. Houses were whitewashed, muddy roads were filled with gravel, and dunghills were removed by official edict. The gates were hung with cloth banners bearing the queen's arms. A special goblet was ordered from London and filled with £40 as a gift to the queen, all in gold coins bearing her image. Though the beautiful ceramic wine jug from Littlecote House was not in fact made especially to entertain Elizabeth, it is typical of the many items that were (figure 49). Manufactured in Germany for the English market, it bears the royal

FIGURE 48. Elizabeth I on progress to Nonsuch Palace, from John Nichols, *The Progresses and Public Processions of Queen Elizabeth* (London, 1823). Case F4549 .626, vol. 1, plate 5. Newberry Library, Chicago.

arms of Elizabeth below the festive, grotesque head that decorates its neck.

The greatest extravaganza, however, came when the queen visited Robert Dudley, earl of Leicester, at Kenilworth (also known as Killingworth). There she spent nineteen days, filled with hunting, feasting, and elaborate entertainments. So intense was the public interest that an "eyewitness" account was produced, in the form of a letter from an officer of the court to his merchant friend back in London, and rushed into print as Elizabeth returned (figure 50). For Leicester the events were stupendously expensive, but they cemented his position as the queen's favorite host.

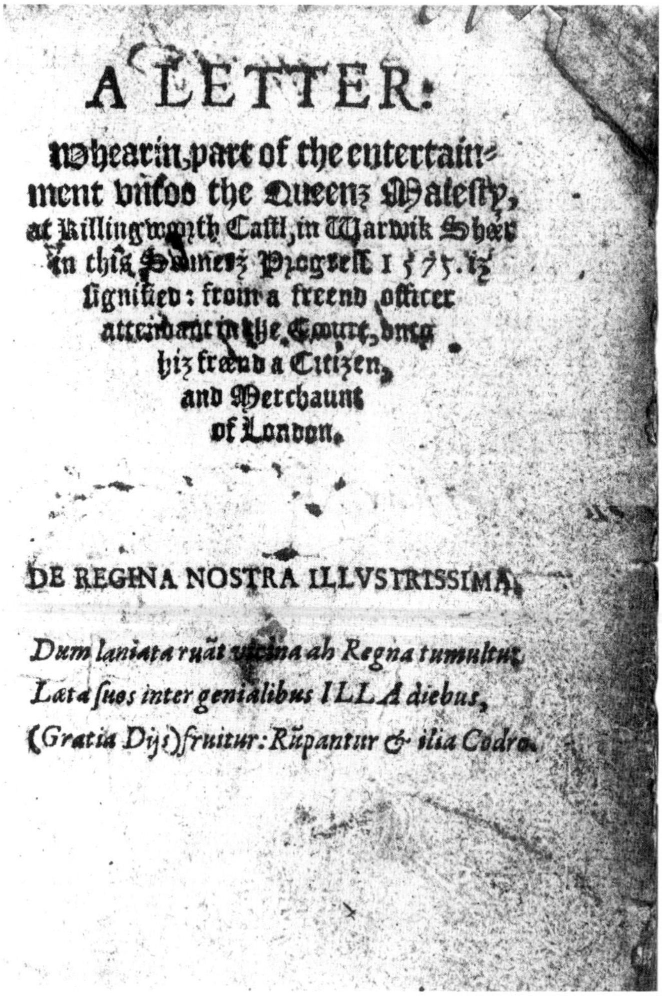

A LETTER:
Whearin, part of the entertainment untoo the Queenz Majesty, at Killingwoorth Castl, in Warwik Sheer in this Soomerz Progress 1575. iz signified: from a freend officer attendant in the Court, untoo hiz freend a Citizen, and Merchaunt of London.

DE REGINA NOSTRA ILLVSTRISSIMA.

Dum laniata ruat vicina ah Regna tumultu,
Læta suos inter genialibus ILLA diebus,
(Gratia Dijs) fruitur: Rūpantur & ilia Codro.

FIGURE 50. Title page from Ro. La. [Robert Laneham], *A Letter: Whearein, part of the entertainment untoo the Queens Majesty, at Killingwoorth Castl, in Warwik Sheer in this Soomers Progress 1575. is signified* (London, 1575). Case F4549 .478. Newberry Library, Chicago.

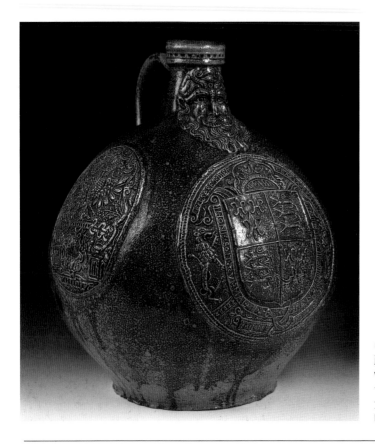

FIGURE 49. German ceramic jug from Littlecote House, with arms of Elizabeth I, 1594. Stoneware, height 35.6 cm. Mr. and Mrs. John H. Bryan.

but no one else imagined he could. Elizabeth saw that she didn't really need a husband, and gradually the nation came to agree. By the time of her last serious courtship, with the duc d'Alençon in 1579 (figure 51), the very people who had begged her to marry twenty years earlier now were begging her not to. Telling Elizabeth she shouldn't marry was as dangerous as telling her she should. Sir Philip Sidney wrote a letter outlining the arguments against the marriage, which circulated discreetly in manuscript. He was sent off to the country to write poetry and reconsider his behavior. One John Stubbs was less discreet and published *The Discoverie of a Gaping Gulf Whereinto England is like to be Swallowed by an other French mariage, if the Lord forbid not the banes, by letting her Majestie see the sin and punishment thereof* (figure 52). Stubbs paid for his act by having the right hand with which he wrote the book hacked off by the executioner. With the other he raised his hat and proclaimed his loyalty to the queen. For Elizabeth, it was a public relations disaster.

It is hard to know how serious the Alençon courtship was. Elizabeth was in her late forties and unlikely to have children without peril of her life. Alençon brought little to the match except his royal lineage. The nation was against it. In any event, she sent him home in 1582, and in 1584 he died. Elizabeth wrote a plaintive letter to Alençon's mother, Catherine de Medici, claiming, incredibly, that her grief was equal to Catherine's own (figure 53). The general reaction is more accurately reflected by an anonymous manuscript poem copied out by the Cambridge scholar Gabriel Harvey. The poem describes how death comes to us all:

> The good, & bad he overtakes, and overthrows in fight.
> The simple swaine, & puissant foreigner are subject to his call:
> Nor Shepherds Cote, nor Princes Court, may ought prevail at all.[42]

"Foreigner" is crossed out, but carefully so that it can still be read, and "Duke" is written in above (figure 54). Through this subtle but transparently phony revision, Harvey's poem laughs from a safe distance at the death of the foreign duke.

Marriage in the sixteenth century meant the subjugation of a woman to a man, and in the end Elizabeth was not going to put up with that. After she died, Sir Robert Naunton claimed that she had said, "I will have here but one mistress and no master."[43] Whether she ever said those words out loud or not, Elizabeth must by this point have realized the truth of what the discerning Scottish ambassador James Melville had said to her: "Your Majesty thinks, if you were marrie'd you would be but Queen of *England*; and now you are both King and Queen."[44]

Though Elizabeth never married, we must still wonder whether the virgin queen was a virgin, or what sort of virgin. In its most basic meaning, the word simply designates a

FIGURE 51. After François Clouet, *Duc d'Alençon,* from Frederick Chamberlain, *The Sayings of Queen Elizabeth* (London: John Lane, 1923). E5 .E43204, plate 2. Newberry Library, Chicago.

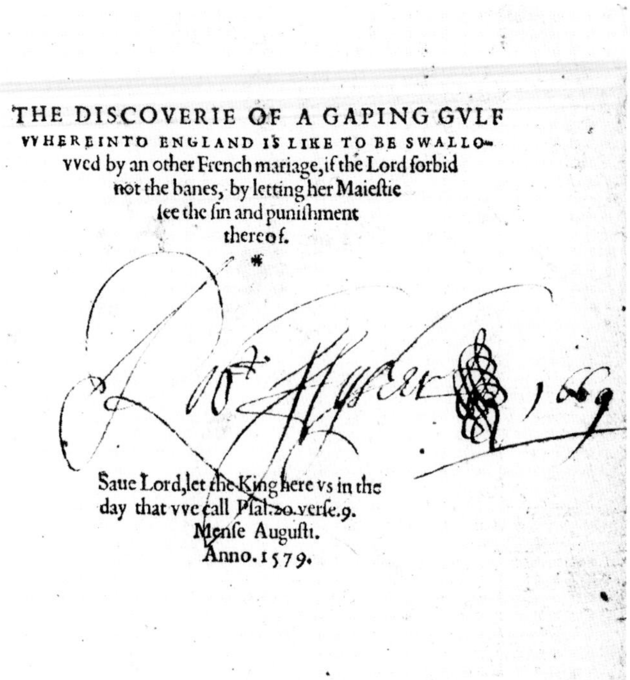

THE DISCOVERIE OF A GAPING GVLF
VVHEREINTO ENGLAND IS LIKE TO BE SWALLO-
vved by an other French mariage, if the Lord forbid
not the banes, by letting her Maieftie
fee the fin and punifhment
thereof.

Saue Lord, let the King here vs in the
day that vve call Pfal.20.verfe.9.
Menfe Augufti.
Anno. 1579.

FIGURE 52. Title page from John Stubbs, *The Discoverie of a Gaping Gulf Whereinto England is Like to be Swallowed by an other French mariage, if the Lord forbid not the banes, by letting her Majestie see the sin and punishment thereof* (N.p., 1579). Case 3A .2106. Newberry Library, Chicago.

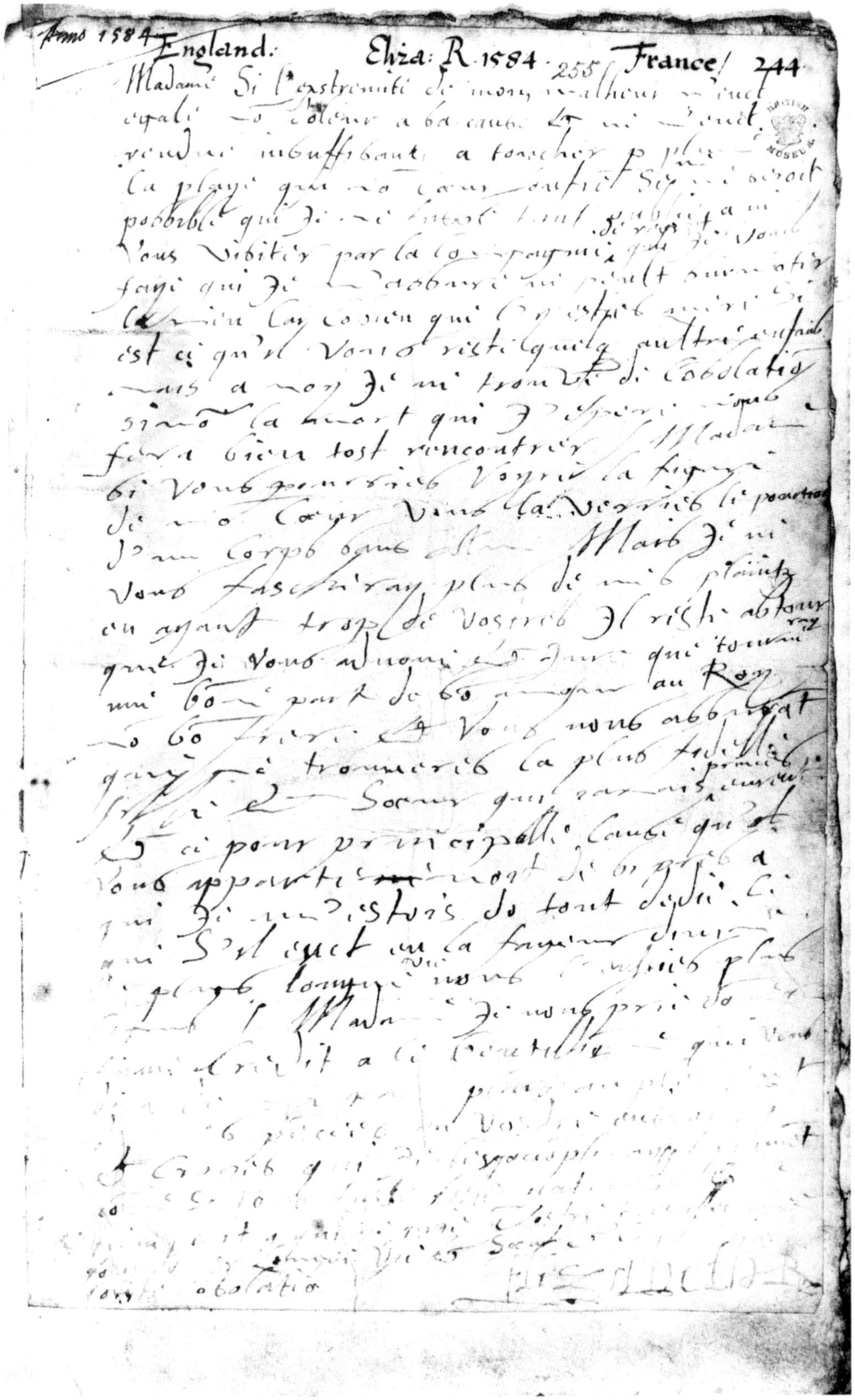

FIGURE 53. Elizabeth I, letter to Catherine de Medici on the death of Duc d'Alençon, circa July 1584. MS Cotton Galba E. VI, fol. 255r. Reproduced by permission of the British Library.

young woman who isn't married and hasn't had any ill-timed pregnancies or scandals that ruin her chances on the marriage market. She is under the control of her father or brother or male next-of-kin, and if some fellow messes with her, he is messing with them, since her sexual behavior affects their honor and their property. As a queen regnant, Elizabeth was in an altogether unusual circumstance. There was no father or brother to intrude. The consequences of her actions would fall first and foremost on her alone in the form of inconvenient babies, scandal, or death in childbirth.

Did Elizabeth have sex? A fair number of Elizabethans thought she did. The episode with Seymour had first raised public rumors. Others thought—and sometimes even said out loud—that, after she was queen, she went on summer progresses away from London in order to give birth to her illegitimate babies, who then were burned.[45] Once past the adolescent adventure of Seymour, Elizabeth may have been too wise to take the risks of a consummated sexual relationship. But in circumstances where full intercourse was very dangerous, people become remarkably inventive. She was healthy and attractive, had been raised in a court with more than its share of licentiousness, and was surrounded by handsome men eager to please her. Once she had reached her forties, Elizabeth seems to have accepted the idea of being the Virgin Queen. But up until then, she may well have sampled the alternatives.

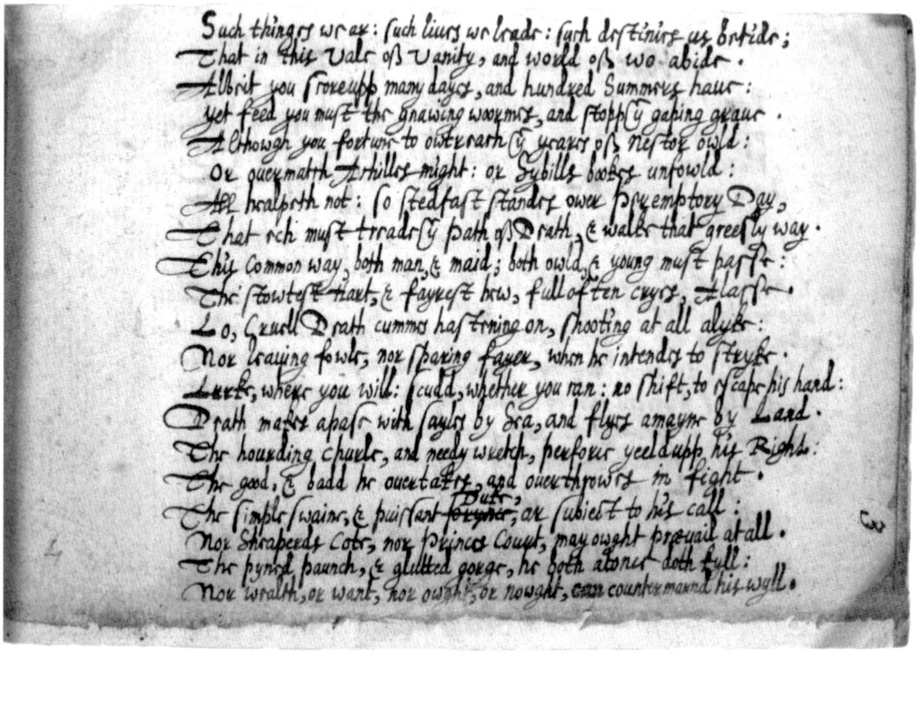
Such thinges wee: such liues we leade: such destinies us betide;
That in this Vale of Vanity, and world of wo abide.
Albeit you sroteupp many dayes, and hundred Summers haue:
yet feed you must the gnawing woormes, and stopp the gaping graue.
Although you fortune to ouerreach the yeares of Nestor owld:
Or ouermatch Achilles might: or Sybills bookes unfowld:
All healpeth not: so stedfast standes ower peremptory Day,
That wee must treade the path of Death, & walke that greesly way.
This common way, both man, & maid; both owld, & young must passe:
The stowtest hart, & fayrest hew, full often cryes, Alasse.
Lo, Cruell Death cummes hastening on, shooting at all alyke:
Nor leauing fowle, nor sparing fayer, when he intendes to stryke.
Lurke, where you will: scudd, whether you ran: no shift, to escape his hand:
Death makes apase with sayles by Sea, and flyes amayne by Land.
The hoording churle, and needy wretch, perforce yeeldupp his Right:
The good, & badd he ouertakes, and ouerthrowes in fight.
The simple swaine, & puissant Duke, are subiect to his call:
Nor Shepeards Cote, nor Princes Court, may ought preuail at all.
The pyned paunch, & glutted gorge, he both atones doth fyll:
Nor wealth, or want, nor ought, or nought, can countermand his wyll.

FIGURE 54. Anonymous, "A View, or Spectacle of Vanity," from Gabriel Harvey, autograph manuscript of a portion of a commonplace book, circa 1584. Uncataloged. Courtesy of the Rare Book and Special Collections Library, University of Illinois at Urbana-Champaign.

FIGURE 55. Sheldon Tapestry Works, Barcheston, England, "Susanna and the Elders," circa 1600. Colored wools and silks with metallic threads, 55.9 × 104.1 cm. Mr. and Mrs. John H. Bryan.

More important in the long run is what Elizabeth's refusal to marry meant for other women. She did not advance other women to formal office, nor did she espouse anything resembling a modern idea of women's emancipation. But her example spoke loudly, and other women saw in her a model for self-determination. This is widely reflected in the art forms dominated at the time by women, such as embroidery. For instance, a beautiful embroidered cushion cover of around 1600 takes as its theme the story of Susanna and the Elders, from the biblical Apocrypha (figure 55). In the left panel, Susanna goes to bathe; in the center panel, the elders of the temple spy Susanna bathing, and attempt to have sex with her. In the right panel, she stands before the judge falsely accused of trying to seduce them, and is rescued by the angel of the Lord. The thematic of female innocence and resistance was widespread in works created by women, and in those created for women. In Elizabeth they found their living symbol.

Elizabeth the Indian Queen

When Sir Walter Raleigh journeyed in 1595 into the South American interior, he encountered a woman ruler of the "Canuri" people, "who came [from] afar off to see our nation, and asked me divers questions of her Majesty, being much delighted with the discourse of her Majesty's greatness and wondering at such reports as we truly made of her Highness' many virtues."[1]

Raleigh's meeting with the leader of the Canuri, which he recounts in *The Discoverie of Guiana* (1596), establishes female rule as a feature that the English thought they shared with the indigenous peoples of South America. Raleigh imagines that Eliza-

beth could not only establish English supremacy in his "Guiana" (present-day Venezuela), but also form an alliance with the Incas and lead Native Americans in their resistance against the empire of Spain.

The vision of Elizabeth as an Indian Queen is captured in two striking images. The first is a painting from around 1600 showing Elizabeth riding under a canopy during a procession (figure 56). The second image comes from Theodor De Bry's *America* (1590) and is uncannily similar to the painting in its depiction of a Native American queen being carried in a litter by her attendants (figure 57).

FIGURE 56. Robert Peake (attributed), *Queen Elizabeth I Being Carried in Procession*, circa 1600. Oil on canvas, 132 × 190.5 cm. Private collection/Bridgeman Art Library.

37

FIGURE 57. Indian queen in procession, from Theodor De Bry, *Brevis Narratio . . . Americæ* [Brief narration . . . of America] (Frankfurt, 1591). Ayer *110 .B9 1590a, vol. 2, plate 37. Newberry Library, Chicago.

Raleigh describes Guiana itself as if the land were a woman "that hath yet her maidenhead, never sacked, turned, nor wrought."[2] The virgin land is in his mind a lot like the Virgin Queen, and in each case it is unclear whether he is more interested in protecting it or exploiting it. In any case, Raleigh's colonial enterprise in Guiana was even less successful than the settlement he briefly established on the North American coast. As for Elizabeth, she was named *weroanza,* or supreme chief, in 1586 by a small group of Algonquins who were friendly to Raleigh's Virginia colony. But the dream of a broader alliance with Native Americans proved to be a tragic fantasy.

—Jonathan Walker

NOTES

1. Sir Walter Raleigh, *The Discoverie of the Large, Rich, and Bewtiful Empyre of Guiana* (London, 1596), p. 91.
2. Ibid., p. 96.

SEDITION AND SUCCESSION

Elizabeth's struggles with the marriage question were inseparable from the succession question. Indeed, her problem was simply the inverse of her father's problem. He created confusion over the succession by marrying so often. She created confusion by not marrying at all. The internal political crises of Elizabeth's reign can be seen as a single long crisis over who would come after her. This crisis lasted from the moment she came to the throne to the moment of her death.

The succession question was also tied up with Mary Queen of Scots (figure 58). Nine years younger than Elizabeth, she was the granddaughter of Henry VIII's older sister Margaret, who had married James IV of Scotland. Her father, James V, had married the French noblewoman Mary of Guise, and Mary herself—as the child monarch of Scotland—was raised in the French royal court, while her mother was regent in Scotland. (See "The Royal House of Tudor," the genealogical table on pages xx–xxi.)

When Elizabeth came to the throne of England, Mary announced her own claim. Since Mary had no army to back it up with, all she managed was to annoy Elizabeth. Her claim did, however, put England and Europe on notice that if Elizabeth died childless, Mary would give it a second try. And while Elizabeth hesitated about marriage, Mary wed the king of France. When he died, she married again, this time to Henry Stuart, Lord Darnley, an English nobleman who himself boasted of royal descent. In time, they had a son, James.

FIGURE 58. After François Clouet, *Mary Queen of Scots,* late nineteenth century. Tempera on ivory, 5 × 4 cm. Case oDA787 .A3 .P7, no. 1. Newberry Library, Chicago.

Up through the moment in June 1566 when James was born, Mary had succeeded in doing the two things that most Englishmen wanted Elizabeth to do. She was married. She had a child and heir. But the rest of Mary's life was already providing evidence for Elizabeth of what could happen to a queen at the hands of the men around her. First Mary entered into a deadly contest with her husband. In March 1566, Darnley had instigated the killing of Mary's court favorite, the musician David Rizzio (with whom Mary was perhaps having a fling). In retaliation, Darnley was assassinated in February 1567. Some historians still exonerate Mary, but the overwhelming verdict, both then and now, is that she was deeply involved in the murder. And then—in what is surely one of the most colossal pieces of political bad judgment anywhere ever—she married her husband's killer, the earl of Bothwell. Her enemies rose in outraged rebellion, and Mary—as if to outdo herself in folly—fled across the border into England.

At the age of twenty-five, Mary had thrown away a crown that had been hers since she was one week old, and had landed herself at the gates of a monarch whom she had already tried once to supplant. For Elizabeth, this was the best and worst of worlds. Her chief rival was within her power. But her chief rival was also within her borders, and Elizabeth herself and her capital were within marching distance of any rebel army that might prefer to have the pliant, marriageable, and Catholic Mary on the throne.

The first serious attempt came in 1569, at the hands of Thomas Howard, duke of Norfolk. He was Elizabeth's cousin on her mother's side, and the leading aristocrat in England. A Protestant with Catholic sympathies and relations, he was the obvious and ideal match for Mary who, despite her later reputation as a martyr to Catholicism, had often compromised with the Scottish Protestants. Nobles and councilors from all sides secretly urged Norfolk to marry the Scottish queen and so make her suitable for England. Some were hoping to put them on the throne, since Elizabeth's confrontations with Parliament had convinced them that she was never going to marry. Others no doubt were hoping for Norfolk's destruction.

The planning and maneuvering went on for months, and Elizabeth must have known all about it, since both Leicester, her favorite, and Cecil, her chief minister, also knew all about it. Finally she confronted Norfolk and ordered him to stop. In the confusion that followed, most of Norfolk's friends scurried for safety. In the north of England, on the Scottish border, the Catholic earls of Northumberland and Westmoreland took up arms and marched around more than enough to commit treason. The conspirators were indecisive and divided in their purposes: some simply wanted to restore Catholicism, some wanted influence over Elizabeth, some wanted to prepare for the time after Elizabeth, and some wanted to kill and replace her right away. In contrast, Elizabeth and her government were relatively decisive: troops were put into the field, and the conspirators and their followers were rounded up and sent home, imprisoned, or executed.

Norfolk himself and his chief ally, Henry Fitzalan, twelfth earl of Arundel, survived for the moment. But it did not end there. One Roberto Ridolfi was weaving a plot to rescue Mary, kill Elizabeth, and land Spanish troops to secure power over England. The plot required participation from Spain, the papacy, Norfolk, and Mary herself. When the government got wind of it, the political advisors of Mary and Norfolk were hauled in for interrogation, and Elizabeth herself signed the warrant to torture them.

The warrant gives a fascinating glimpse into the Elizabethan mind. It is written out by William Cecil, an outstanding scholar turned chief minister; signed by Elizabeth; and addressed to two of England's leading humanists: Sir Thomas Smith, afterward a member of the queen's Privy Council and author of the most important book of English political theory of its time, and Sir Thomas Wilson, a leading court official and author of the standard works on rhetoric and logic that were read by any aspiring lawyer, diplomat, or poet, including the queen herself. The copy of Wilson's *The rule of Reason* in a binding with Elizabeth's arms—and presumably from her library—is a well-thumbed book attesting to heavy use (figure 59). Likewise, those to be tortured—Norfolk's secretaries—were men of intellect and learning. (One had just served as a member of Parliament.) They, like their torturers and the queen who directs the torture, all embody the virtues and qualities that we associate with the humanism of the Renaissance.

FIGURE 59. Leather binding with royal arms of Elizabeth I, from Thomas Wilson, *The rule of Reason, conteinyng the Arte of Logique* (London, 1551). Case B49 .976. Newberry Library, Chicago.

Renaissance Humanism

The word "humanism" often has a fuzzy meaning for us, denoting something like a concern for others. During Elizabeth's lifetime it had a quite precise meaning as "the study of what makes us human," as opposed to the study of nature or divinity.

Humanistic study included history, law, ancient and modern languages, and literature. Humanists sought to reform these subjects to reflect more accurately the truth of nature and the wisdom achieved by ancient Greece and Rome. This led to what they believed was a "renaissance" or rebirth of learning in their time, and led them to dismiss the intervening centuries as a "dark" or "middle" age.

The reform of learning reached into every area of life. It began with the editing of classical texts, and then reached to changes in grammar, logic, and writing style to follow the classical models. History, poetry, drama, architecture, art, and philosophy were refashioned along humanist lines. Even the shapes of letters were changed to correspond to what seemed the best examples from the past. A young person receiving a humanist education would learn reading, writing, ethics, history, and languages simultaneously by copying, imitating, and refashioning the models set before him (figure 60).

Humanists did not imagine that their new learning was intended just for private cultivation or recreation. They expected it to have an impact on public life. Because of their knowledge of languages, law, and history, humanists were in high demand as government officials and diplomats. For a smart young male in Tudor England, a humanist education at Cambridge or Oxford or at the Inns of Court was a road to advancement. Edmund Spenser made his living in govern-

FIGURE 60. "Q," from John Scottowe, "Calligraphic Alphabet," 1592. Wing MS ZW 545 .S431. Newberry Library, Chicago.

ment while awaiting recognition as a poet, and Thomas Wilson and Thomas Smith rose to positions on Elizabeth's Privy Council.

Aristocrats were also expected to internalize humanist ideals, not only through formal education but also through a new standard of civilized behavior. *The Courtier,* published in 1528 by the Italian humanist Baldassare Castiglione, describes this ideal. It was wildly influential across Europe and adopted by the middle class as well. Castiglione's work was translated into English by Cecil's brother-in-law Thomas Hoby in 1561. The copy illustrated here belonged to Edmund Spenser's friend Gabriel Harvey, a scholar at Cambridge (figure 61). Harvey dreamed of a life of power and influence at court, but his fate was to remain at Cambridge. He was not alone in finding that reconciling humanist learning with humane conduct was a difficult and sometimes elusive goal.

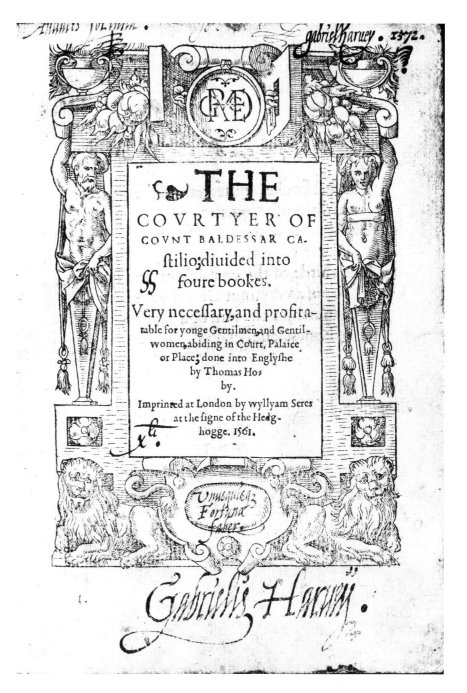

FIGURE 61. Title page from Gabriel Harvey's copy of Thomas Hoby, *The Courtyer of Count Baldessar Castilio* (London, 1561). Case Y712 .C27495. Newberry Library, Chicago.

The warrant lays out what reasonable people can do to one another. Smith and Wilson are given the power to do whatever they think is appropriate "for knowledge of the truth." As if they were still schoolteachers dealing with their students, they are to give "an examination of them upon all points." The examination proceeds in stages: they will be "put to the rack" and then "taste thereof," and so forth, until they "confess plainly their knowledge."[46] The ideal of humanism is to know oneself by looking inside, and to explain that inner truth plainly to the world. Here, ironically, the ideal of humanism is acted out in physical terms, with pain and suffering.

Evidence in hand, the government launched a campaign to change public opinion about both Mary and Norfolk. A treatise denouncing Mary written in Latin several years before by the great Scottish scholar George Buchanan was translated into English by Wilson and published, along with letters (the so-called "Casket Letters") that incriminated Mary in the murder of her husband, Darnley (figure 62). Norfolk's own involvement in the English conspiracy and rebellion was announced to the citizens of London and likewise laid out in print.

On July 2, 1572, Norfolk was executed. For Arundel there was mercy. He was confined and eventually forced into retirement (figure 63). With them went the power of two ancient families who had been part of the ruling elite for far longer than the Tudors (though both families would recover under the Stuarts). After Norfolk, Elizabeth would have no more dukes. There would continue to be earls and so forth, but she kept a vacant space between herself and the loftiest noble.

But Mary still lived, still claimed the throne of Scotland, and still was next in blood to the throne of England. For the next dozen years she remained penned up, trying to negotiate or murder her way out. The negotiations involved an assortment of plans. One was that she would formally abdicate the throne of Scotland in favor of her son, James, if Elizabeth would formally name James as her successor. It is hard to imagine that either queen really wanted to make this bargain. But the go-betweens loyally tried to make a deal. In 1584, for instance, Mary's secretary, Claude Nau, wrote to Robert Beale, the secretary to the Privy Council (figure 64). Could Beale persuade Cecil (now Lord Burghley) to persuade Elizabeth to write Mary a nice letter and improve her conditions of confinement? At the same time, Nau would try to persuade Mary to write, but she had a cramp in her hand—caused by the poor conditions. This surely was a diplomatic illness. Compliments and expressions of concern flowed on all sides, and the negotiations went nowhere.

So the alternative was murder. Mary's letter approving of an assassination plot by one Anthony Babington was intercepted. In autumn 1586, Mary was tried for treason before a special court and convicted. Elizabeth was reluctant to impose the mandatory

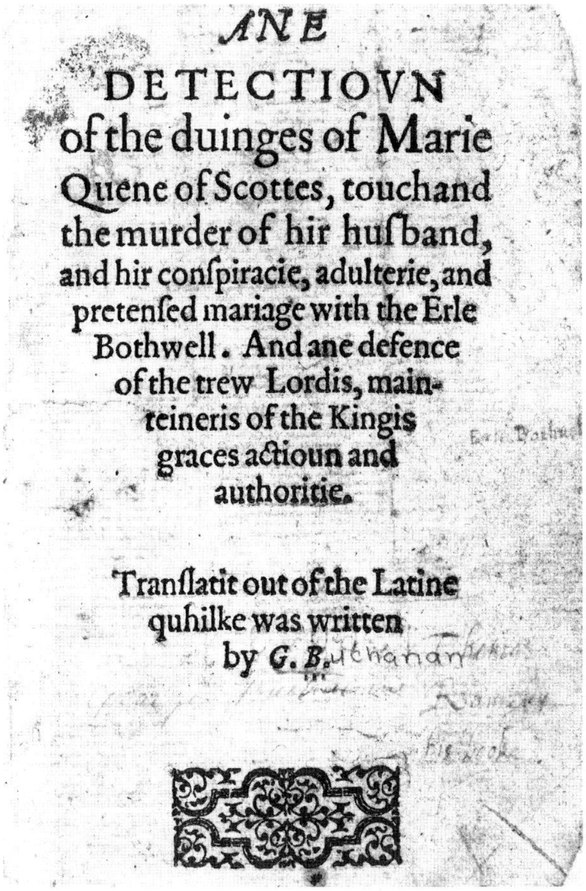

ANE

DETECTIOVN

of the duinges of Marie
Quene of Scottes, touchand
the murder of hir hufband,
and hir confpiracie, adulterie, and
pretenfed mariage with the Erle
Bothwell. And ane defence
of the trew Lordis, main-
teineris of the Kingis
graces actioun and
authoritie.

Tranflatit out of the Latine
quhilke was written
by G. B.

FIGURE 62. Title page from George Buchanan, *Ane Detectioun of the duinges of Marie Quene of Scottes* (London, 1572). Bonaparte 12035. Newberry Library, Chicago.

FIGURE 63. Oak armchair with arms of the Arundel family, circa 1570, height 101.5 cm. Mr. and Mrs. John H. Bryan.

89

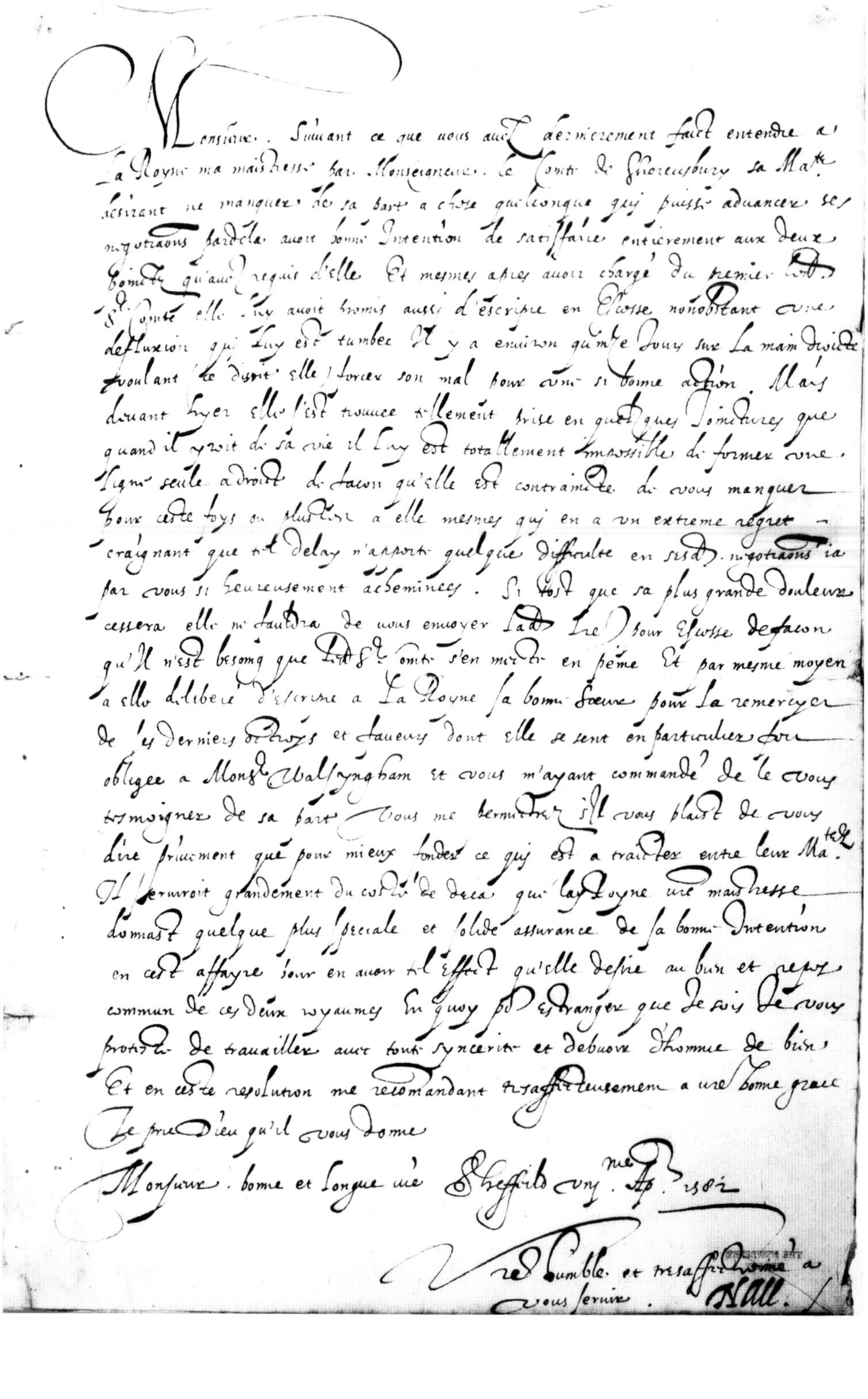

death sentence. As a practical politician, she was deeply concerned about international reaction. After all, Mary was the queen of a sovereign nation, and, then as now, there were rules about killing other people's rulers. As an anointed queen, Elizabeth hardly wanted to suggest that killing anointed queens, even bad ones, was a good idea. And there was the memory of the execution of another anointed queen, Elizabeth's own mother, Anne Boleyn.

Parliament petitioned her to execute Mary, for its safety and for Elizabeth's. On November 12, 1586, she put the members off with fair words. Twelve days later they petitioned again, and she delivered one of her most famous speeches of hesitation, telling them she was simply not ready to decide, and sent them away with an "answer answerless."

Again the government prepared its case in print. The most common way of communicating important political news was by private letter, and the best letters full of gossip and insider information were often copied and shared with others. Elizabeth's councilors now prepared a very public document entitled *The Copie of a Letter to the Right Honourable the Earle of Leycester . . . With a report of certaine petitions and declarations made to the Queenes Majestie at two severall times . . . And her Majesties answeres thereunto by her selfe delivered* from one "R.C.," obviously Robert Cecil, the son of Lord Burghley (figure 65). Cecil wrote a narrative of the trial itself and the evidence. To it were added his own edited transcripts of Parliament's pleas to Elizabeth and the queen's replies, carefully polished up by the queen herself (figure 66). The touches are pure Elizabeth. The homespun wish that she and Mary "were but as two milkmaids with pails under our arms" is changed to "pails upon our arms."[47] At other times Elizabeth's anger lashes out in the phrasing she used during her girlhood dangers, when she warns that her initial leniency was not some "simplicity, or want of understanding."[48]

The book was printed with clearly marked royal approval in English, and then in French, German, Dutch, and Latin. It was a battle not just for English opinion, but for the opinion of all Europe. And from behind the scenes, Elizabeth clearly was directing it.

Two months later, on February 8, 1587, Mary was executed. The warrant was carried from London to Fotheringay, where Mary was kept captive, by Robert Beale, who years earlier had corresponded with Claude Nau on behalf of the Privy Council. Once Mary was dead, the news was reported back both visually and verbally. The sketch from Beale's papers (figure 67) shows the event in stages. From a doorway at the upper left, the veiled Mary is led out, trailed by her ladies in waiting. Around the platform stand the onlookers, with the official witnesses seated at the top and to the left. At the lower center of the platform, the Scottish queen takes off her outer garments, again helped by her

7

A SHORT EXTRACT OF

such reasons, as were deliuered in speach by Master Sergeant Puckering, Speaker of the Lower House, before the Queenes most excellent Maiestie in her Presence Chamber at Richmond, the xii. of Nouember 1586. in the xxviii. yeere of her Reigne, containing diuers apparant and imminent dangers, that may grow to her Maiesties most Royal person, and to her Realme from the Scottish Queene and her Adherents, if remedie be not prouided.

¶ First, touching the danger of her Maiesties person.

1 Both this Scottish Queene and her fauourers, doe thinke her to haue right, not to succeed but to enioy your Crowne in possession: and therefore as shee is a most impacient competitor, so will shee not spare any meanes whatsoeuer, that may bereaue vs of your Maiestie, the onely impediment that shee enioyeth not her desire.

2 Shee is obdurate in malice against your royall person, notwithstanding you haue shewed her all fauour and mercie, as well in preseruing her kingdome, as sauing her life, and saluing her honour. And therefore there is no place for mercie, since there is no hope that shee will desist from most wicked attempts: the rather for that her malice appeareth such, that shee maketh (as it were) her testament of the same, to be executed after her death, and appoynteth her executors to performe it.

3 Shee

8

3 Shee boldly and openly professed it lawfull for her to mooue inuasion vpon you. And therefore, as of inuasion victorie may ensue, and of victorie, the death of the vanquished: so did shee thereby not obscurely bewraie, that shee thought it lawfull for her to destroie your sacred person.

4 Shee thinkes it not onely lawfull, but honourable also and meritorious to take your life from you, as being alreadie depriued of your Crowne by the excommunication of the holie father. And therefore it is like shee will (as hitherto shee hath done) continually seeke it by whatsoeuer meanes.

5 That shee is greedie of your Maiesties death, and preferreth it before her owne life and safetie: for in her direction to one of her late Complices, shee aduised (vnder couert termes) that whatsoeuer should become of her, that tragicall execution should be performed vpon you.

1 It is most perillous to spare her, that continually hath sought the ouerthrow and suppression of true Religion, infected with Poperie from her tender youth, and being after that a Confederate in that Holy league when shee came to age, and euer since a professed enemie against the trueth. *The danger of the ouerthrow of the true Religion.*

2 She resteth wholly vpon Popish hopes to deliuer and aduance her, and is thereby so deuoted to that profession, that aswell for satisfaction of others, as for feeding of her owne humor, shee will supplant the Gospell, where, and when so euer shee may: which euill is so much the greater, and the more to be auoyded, as that it stay-

B.iij.   eth

ladies in waiting. Finally, at the upper right of the platform, the executioner chops off her head. Written accounts came back from those present, including the official witnesses, the earls of Kent and Shrewsbury. To supplement the drawing, Beale then drafted the written report. The original copy of course went to the council. But Beale, again, made his own copy, and must have shared it with others (figure 68).

Elizabeth's role has been hotly debated by historians. She sent the warrant, and then called it back, but somehow not in time. Those responsible for the execution were disciplined, but not very much. In short, she matched her "answer answerless" of November with the "order orderless" of February, and distanced herself, just barely, from the most scandalous action of her regime.

Not everyone believed her. On the Continent, the act was roundly condemned. "I never saw a thing more hated by little, great, old, young and of all religions than the Queen of Scots' death, and especially the manner of it," wrote Sir Robert Stafford, the English ambassador in France.[49] From Scotland came protests by King James over the death of his mother. James's personal letter to Elizabeth is filled with corrections and revisions, and left unsigned, as if written in extreme haste and agitation (figure 69). He weighs Elizabeth's denial of responsibility for the death of Mary, noting Elizabeth's rank, sex, closeness in blood, and "long-professed good will to the defunct," together with her "many and solemn attestations of your innocence." He then says he will judge her innocence on the basis of her future actions and "proof of your honorable and kind dealings" in their efforts to "strengthen and unite this isle."[50] In short, he will believe her innocence if she will make him king of England. It is a remarkable diplomatic performance, interweaving personal feeling with political calculation.

Comparisons between Elizabeth and Mary are inevitable, and continue to our day. Elizabeth gained a throne and Mary lost one, each at the age of twenty-five. This testifies to the opposite skills that they acquired in their first quarter-century of life. One learned prudence, judgment, and diplomacy and developed an exquisite sense of timing. The other innately possessed or carefully developed a self-absorption and exquisitely bad judgment. Mary succeeded at only one thing, which was producing an heir. Elizabeth succeeded at everything else.

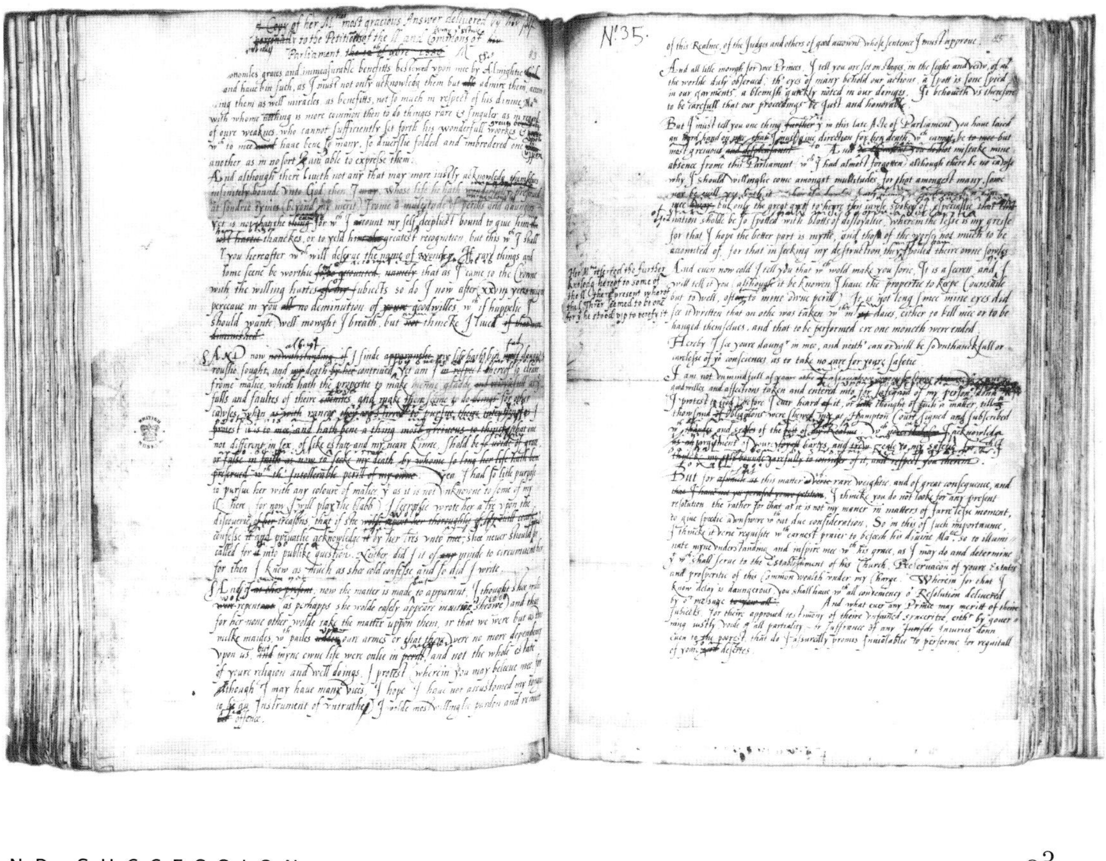

FIGURE 66. Elizabeth I, speech to Parliament concerning Mary Queen of Scots, November 12, 1586. MS Lansdowne 94, art. 35A, fols. 84v–85r. Reproduced by permission of the British Library.

FIGURE 67. Robert Beale, drawing of the execution of Mary Queen of Scots, 1587. MS Additional 48027, fol. 650*. Reproduced by permission of the British Library.

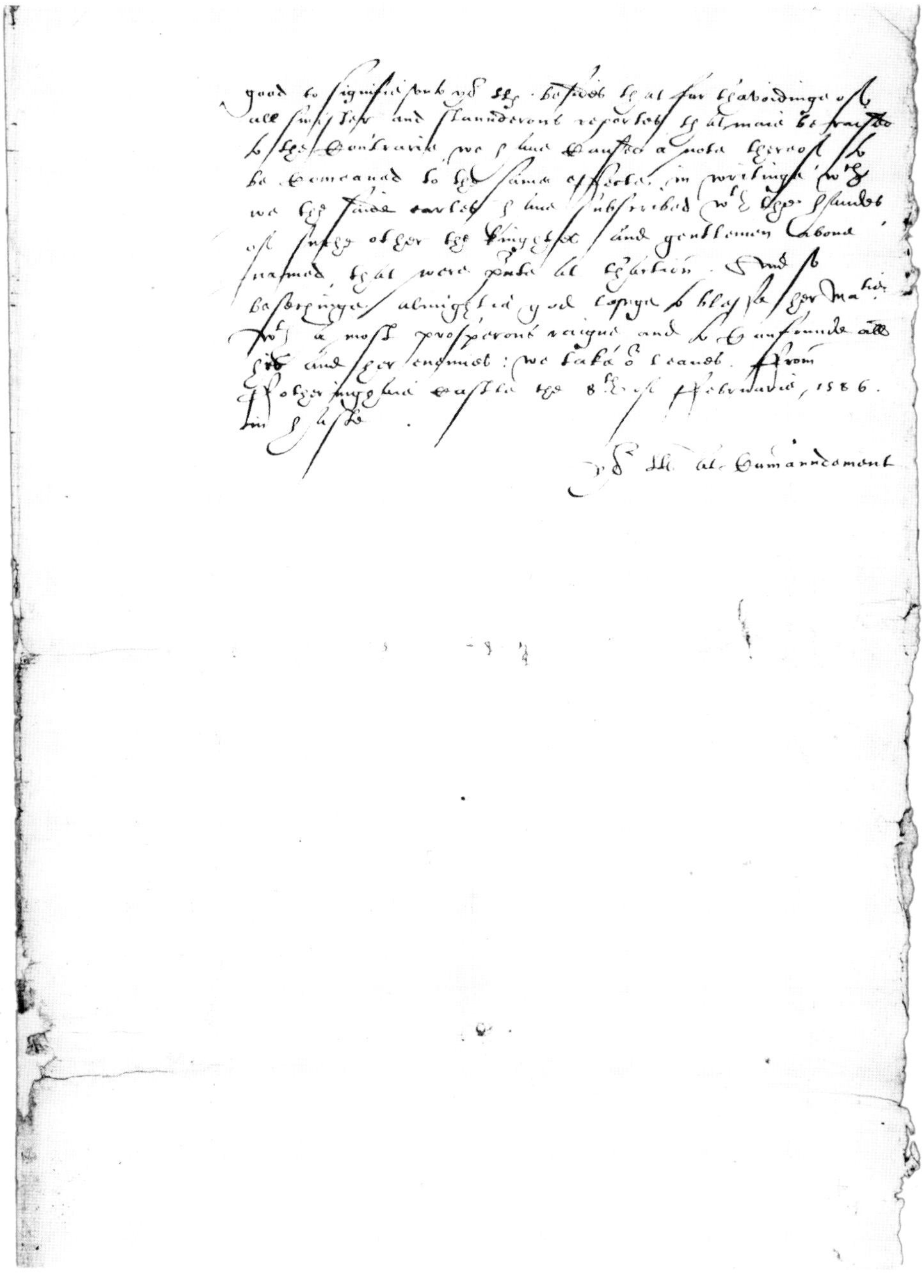

good to signifie vnto vs her behest that for the avoidinge of
all suche false and slanderous reportes as maie be raised
to the Contrarie, we haue caused a note hereof to
be Conveyed to the same effecte, in writinge, wch
we the three earles haue subscribed wth ther handes
of suche other the Knyghtes and gentlemen there aboute
named, that were present at th'action. And so
besechinge almightie god to preserue to hir ma:tie
bothe a most prosperous reigne and to Confounde all
her and her enimies: we take o:r leaue. from
Fotheringhaie castle the 8:th of februarie, 1586.

yo:r lo:ps

                              by hir ma:tie Commaundement

FIGURE 68. Henry Grey, Earl
of Kent, letter to William
Cecil, Lord Burghley, report-
ing the execution of Mary
Queen of Scots, February 8,
1587 (copy by Robert Beale).
Case MS 5089, fol. 3r. Newberry Library, Chicago.

Madame & dearest sister ~~haue receaued~~ youre letair be youre seruand & ambassadoure ~~letteris cares~~ ye purge youre self of one unhappy fact as on the one pairt considdering youre rank & sexe, consanguinitie, & longe professed goode will to the defunct together with youre many & solemne attestationis of youre innocentie I darr not wronge you so farre as not to iudge honorablie of youre unspotted pairt thairin So on the other syde I wishe that youre honorable behauioure in all tymes heirafter may fully persuaide the quhole worlde ~~of youre innocent pairt thairin~~ & as for my pairt I looke that ye will ~~at this tyme~~ geue me at this tyme suche a full satisfaction in all respectis as sall be a meane to s트렌thin & unite this yle, establishe & maintaine the trew religion, & oblis me to be as of before I was youre most louing

this bearare hath langue to informe you of in my name quhom I neid not desyre you to credit for ye knaw stoute him

Dramatists and filmmakers have loved to invent scenes where the two meet. Inevitably, they show the older Elizabeth as bitter, sexually frustrated, and intensely jealous of her younger, taller, prettier, more romantic rival. This is, perhaps, the ultimate male fantasy about both queens. For surely, of the two, it was Elizabeth who had what men want, and that was power. If some seemed to prefer Mary to Elizabeth, it was because Mary kept giving it away, and Elizabeth liked to keep it for herself.

Still, the legend of Elizabeth is haunted by the legend of Mary—or rather, the two legends. One is the legend of Mary as the monarch who died for her faith, loyal to the church of Rome in the face of the Protestant fury of Walsingham, Burghley, and their henchmen. The other is the legend of Mary as the monarch who gave all for love, following her heart and not her head. Both are the subjects of opera, film, and fiction, if not of history.

With the death of Mary, sedition lost its focus, and England faced more threats from abroad than from home. Mary's son, James VI of Scotland, was the presumptive heir. But, as Elizabeth herself had predicted, James too in time became the focal point for conspiracies against her. The most famous and important of these is the revolt of Robert Devereux, earl of Essex, in 1601. The revolt was not directly (or at least openly) in favor of James. But Essex claimed to believe that Cecil and others were planning to put the Spanish infanta on the throne when Elizabeth died, and he rushed to defend the realm against the pretended threat.

The revolt was the sordid end to what had been a close relationship between Elizabeth and Essex for fifteen years. He was the stepson of Robert Dudley, earl of Leicester (Leicester had married Essex's mother after giving up hope of marrying Elizabeth herself.) He was the leading aristocrat of the younger generation, and the darling of the poets, including Shakespeare. Elizabeth showered him with favors and set him up as a rival to Burghley's son Robert Cecil (whom he outshone by birth and bearing but could not match for brains).

Essex's letters to Elizabeth are outpourings of affection. Typical is one written in late 1597 (figure 70): "Most deer Lady, . . . since I was first so happy, as to know what Love meant, I was never one day nor one hour free from hope and jealousy. And as long as you do me right, they are the two inseparable companions of my life. . . . And as wishing your majesty to be Mistress of that you wish most, I humbly kiss your fair hands. Your servant in Love and duty before all men, R. Essex."[51]

By itself this is fine, but it is wrapped around a request that she "do him right" by stopping criticism of his wasteful military expeditions against the Spanish, and stopping her favors to others.

In March 1599 Essex got his big break and was sent with an army to put down the

FIGURE 70. Robert Devereux, Earl of Essex, letter to Elizabeth I, October–November 1597. MS Additional 74286, fol. 99, #36. Reproduced by permission of the British Library.

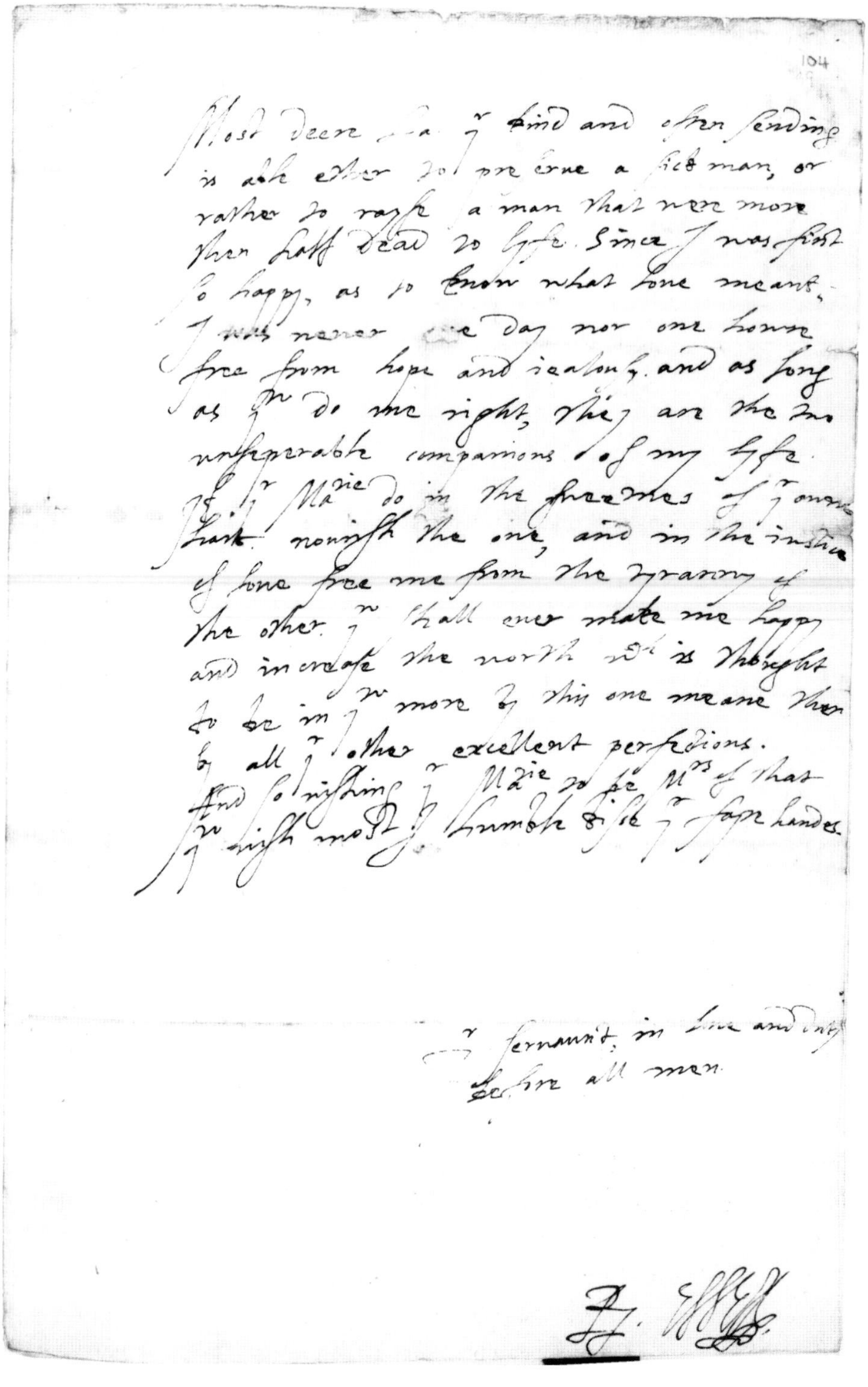

104

Most deere Lady your kind and often sending
is the other day to preserve a sick man, or
rather to rayse a man that were more
then half dead to lyfe. Since I was first
so happy, as to know what love meant,
I was never one day nor one houre
free from hope and iealousy. and as long
as your do me right, they are the
unseperable companions of my lyfe.
If your Matie do in the freenes of your
hart nourish the one, and in the iustice
of love free me from the tyranny of
the other, your shall ever make me happy
and increase the worth which is thought
to be in your more by this one meane then
by all your other excellent perfections.
And so wishing your Matie to be M^rs of that
you wish most I humbly kiss your fayre handes.

Your servant in love and duty
before all men.

R. Essex.

rebellion of the earl of Tyrone in Ireland. It was a disaster. Essex not only failed to catch Tyrone, he ended up cutting a deal with the rebels that would let him bring his army back to England—where he might use it to advance his own power. Elizabeth smelled treason, and Essex was cast into disfavor. Things were not helped when a minor historian named John Hayward published a history of the *Life and raigne of King Henrie the IIII*, with a lavish dedication to Essex (figure 71). Again, Elizabeth thought the worst and interpreted the book as a political satire. "I am Richard II, know ye not that?" she is said to have exclaimed, meaning that Essex was like Henry Bolingbroke, who deposed Richard and became Henry IV.[52]

The crisis came in February 1601. Essex's followers sponsored a performance of Shakespeare's *Richard II* and then tried to seize the city of London and Elizabeth herself. They were quickly turned back, and after a brief siege, Essex surrendered.

Trial and conviction for treason followed swiftly. For all of the claims of later novelists that she loved him, Elizabeth signed the execution warrant with a large, bold hand on February 24, 1601. The next morning he was dead.

As with the executions of the duke of Norfolk and Mary Queen of Scots, the government carefully explained its case in public. This time its publicist was none other than Sir Francis Bacon, the son of Elizabeth's first lord keeper, Sir Nicholas Bacon, already himself England's leading lawyer, eventually lord chancellor himself, and one of the greatest intellects of any time. Bacon had been a follower of Essex in the good days, but now his job was to explain the need for the earl's execution. Essex and his followers had denied that they intended to harm the queen. But with all the powers of his great mind, Bacon sets out to prove in *A Declaration of the Practices & Treasons attempted and committed by Robert late Earle of Essex and his Complices* (figure 72) that they were at worst lying, and at best kidding themselves, since Elizabeth would never have permitted them to succeed, and so they would have had no course open to them except to kill her.

Whatever Essex's real motives, James VI of Scotland clearly believed that Essex was on his side. Once on the throne of England, James rehabilitated the remaining followers of Essex, including Henry Wriothesley, earl of Southampton, who ten years earlier had been a patron for Shakespeare's poetry. Bacon and others were left to squirm, and in 1605 Bacon issued an *Apologie* for his work on the *Declaration of the Practices & Treasons*. In it, he claims that Elizabeth was angry at his first draft, because it kept referring to Essex with the titles and honors that had been stripped from him upon his conviction for treason. Then the work was "perused, weighed, censured, altered, and made almost anew" first by the counselors and then by the queen herself.[53] It is hard to know just where the truth is in this, but if Bacon's account can be trusted, then Elizabeth was once again the final reviser of her own image.

Illuſtriſſimo & honoratiſsimo *Ro-*
berto Comiti Eſſexiæ & Ewe, Comiti Mareſcallo Angliæ, Vicecomiti Hereſordiæ
& Bourchier : Baroni *Ferrariis de Chartley,*
Domino Bourchier & Louein : Regiæ Maieſtati Hyppo-
como : Machinarum bellicarum præfecto : Academiæ Can-
tabrigienſis Cancellario : ordinis Georgiani Equiti aurato :
Sereniſſimæ Domino Reginæ à ſanctioribus conſilijs :
Domino meo plurimum obſeruando.

Ρίςῳ καὶ γενναιοτάτῳ: *optimo & Nobi-*
liſſimo (inquit Euripides *) ex qua*
ſententia tu primus ac ſolus ferè oc-
currebas (illuſtriſsime comes) cuius
nomē ſi Henrici *noſtri fronte radiaret, ipſe & læ-*
tior & tutior in vulgus prodiret. Magnus, ſiquidem
es, & preſenti iudicio, & futuri temporis expecta-
tione : in quo, veluti recuperaſſe nūc oculos, cæca
prius fortuna videri poteſt ; Dum cumulare ho-
noribus eum geſtit, qui omnibus virtutibus eſt in-
ſignitus. Hunc igitur ſi læta fronte, excipere dig-
neris, ſub nominis tui vmbra, (tanquam ſub Aiacis
clipio Teucer *ille* Homericus *) tutiſsime latebit.*
Deus *opt. max. celſitudinem tuam nobis & reique*
publicæ diu ſeruet incolumem : quo nos vt, tam ſi-
de quam armis, potenti tua dextra defenſi, vltique,
diutina cum ſecuritate tum gloria perfruamur.

Honori tuo deditiſſimus,
I, HAYWARDE.

100

THE EFFECT OF
the Euidence giuen, at the feuerall
Arraignments of the late Earls of
Effex and *Southampton*, before
the L. STEVVARD;

And of Sir *Chriftopher Blunt* and
Sir *Charles Dauers*, and others, before great and Honourable Com-
miffioners of *Oyer* and
Determiner.

And of the Anfweres and Defenfes,
which the faid Offendors made for them-
felues; And the Replies made vpon
fuch their Defenfes:

With fome other Circumftances of the
proceedings, as well at the fame
Arraignments as after.

HE two late Earles of *Effex* and *Southampton*, were brought to their triall, the nineteenth of Februarie, eleuen dayes after the Rebellion. At which trial there paffed vpon them 25. Peeres, a greater number then hath bene called in any former prefident. Amongft whom her Maieftie did not forbeare to vfe many that were of neere alliance and blood to the Earle of *Effex*, and fome others, that had their fonnes and heires ap-parant that were of his Company, and followed him

Some queftion was made by the earle of *Effex*, whether he might cha-lenge any of the Peers. But anfwere was made by the Iudges, that the law had that reputatiõ of the Peeres, that it trufted them both without othe and chalenge.

G 3

FIGURE 72. Royal arms and opening text from Francis Bacon, *A Declaration of the Practices & Treasons attempted and committed by Robert late Earle of Essex and his Complices* (London, 1601). Case F4549 .268, fols. G2v–G3r. Newberry Library, Chicago.

After Elizabeth, Who?

In her 1586 reply to Parliament concerning Mary Queen of Scots, Elizabeth stated that "we princes, I tell you, are set on stages in the sight and view of all the world."[1] Within England, the queen could confine the debate over the succession to the throne to the small circle of Parliament and to the shadowy corners of court intrigue. She had no control, however, over the succession debate on the Continent. Especially during Elizabeth's last decades, English exiles and agents of foreign princes had their say in a series of tracts about the succession in England.

In 1569 John Leslie, the Scottish bishop of Ross and a virulent supporter of Mary Queen of Scots, issued a two-part defense of his mistress's rights. Originally in English, each part was translated and reprinted in Latin, French, and Spanish. The second part, *That the Regiment of Women is Conformable to the Law of God and Nature,* is a refutation of John Knox's attack on women rulers, and is considerably stronger than that offered on Elizabeth's behalf by her own bishop, John Aylmer. The first part, *A Defense of the Honor of the Right High, Mighty, and Noble Princess Mary, Queen of Scotland and Dowager of France,* focuses on the claims of the rivals for the throne. The elaborate genealogical chart from the 1580 Latin edition (figure 73) lists the Lady Arabella Stuart and Lady Catherine Grey, as well as Mary herself and her son, James.

In 1594, the English expatriate and Jesuit priest Robert Parsons wrote and printed *A Conference About the Next Succession to the Crowne of Ingland.* (He used the pseudonym "R. Doleman," and mischievously, he dedicated the book to the earl of Essex.) The *Conference* is organized like a modern political talk show, in which eminent European leaders argue over who would be the most suitable ruler after Elizabeth. (The lawyers were real, but the debate a fiction.) The book settles on the eldest daughter of King Philip II of Spain, the infanta Isabel Clara Eugenia, who traced her genealogy back to John of Gaunt. Ironically, when Essex raised his rebellion, he did so on the pretext that the Privy Council was lining up behind the infanta instead of rallying to James of Scotland.

Mere possession of Parsons's book was a treasonable offense in England. As soon as Elizabeth died, the copies came out of the closet, and John Hayward rushed to print with *An Answer to the First Part of a Certaine Conference, Concerning Succession, Published not long since under the name of R. Dolman.* Hayward had gotten into trouble with his *Life and raigne of King Henrie the IIII,* which seemed to praise Essex as a modern Bolingbroke. But in *An Answer,* Hayward set out to defend the claims of James VI of Scotland—safe ground indeed, since James had already been recognized by the council and the Parliament of England as James I of England, and as the only possible successor to the incomparable, if difficult, Elizabeth.

NOTE

1. Queen Elizabeth's Answer to the Petition of the Lords and Commons, November 12, 1586, British Library, MS. Lansdowne 94, art. 35A, fol. 84v, *Elizabeth I: Collected Works,* ed. Leah S. Marcus, Janel Mueller, and Mary Beth Rose (Chicago: University of Chicago Press, 2000), p. 194.

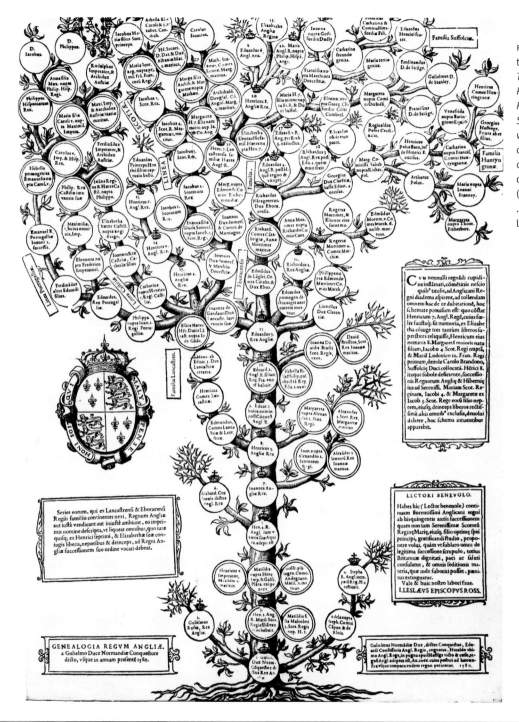

FIGURE 73. Genealogical tree, from John Leslie, *De Titulo et Jure Serenissimæ Principis Mariæ Scotorum Reginæ, quo Regni Angliæ Successionem sibi justè vendicat* [The title and right of Mary, most serene queen of Scots, to the succession of the throne of England] (Rheims, 1580). Case 4A .1828, after ē 4v. Newberry Library, Chicago.

ARMADA

One of the great ironies of her reign is that when Elizabeth made herself safe by executing Mary Queen of Scots, she made herself vulnerable to Philip II of Spain. Philip had good reasons for invading England and deposing Elizabeth. She was the enemy of Philip's religion, and Philip's pope had excommunicated her. In the Spanish Netherlands, her armies had aided the rebels against his power, with her favorite, the earl of Leicester, at their head. In Spanish America, her pirates, especially Sir Francis Drake, had marauded his cities and fleets. So long as Mary lived, he was reluctant to invade, lest he simply put a friend of France on the throne. But Mary dead was another matter. Then she was a justification, a rallying point, and a pretext for his retaliation.

As with the domestic threats, the war was one of words as well as one of swords. Spanish pamphlets traced the origins of the struggle to the marriage of Henry VIII to Elizabeth's mother, Anne Boleyn. The goal of the Armada, according to Padre Pedro de Ribadeneyra, a Spanish Jesuit writing in April 1588, was to end the schism of the English church that had begun with Anne and had led inexorably to the murder of Mary Queen of Scots (figure 74). The Armada itself came in midsummer. The fleet, with 128 ships and 24,000 men, left the coast of Spain on July 12, 1588. Their intent was to link up at Dunkirk with the duke of Parma's army numbering an additional 30,000 men, and then cross the narrow seas to make an amphibious landing on the coast of England.

The English prepared as best they could. Lord Burghley used the margins of his proofsheets from Christopher Saxton's *Atlas of England and Wales* to tally up the strengths and weaknesses (figure 75). In one margin he would list the most likely landing places for Spanish forces. In the other went the queen's munitions and men for each county. It was a piecemeal defense, made vulnerable by a long coastline. Lord Charles Howard of Effingham, the admiral of Elizabeth's fleet, made ready with the aid of his celebrated commanders Sir Francis Drake, Sir John Hawkins, and Sir Martin Frobisher. Simultaneously, Leicester struggled to prepare the army.

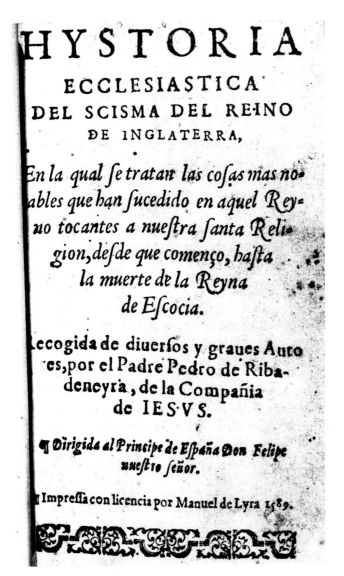

FIGURE 74. Title page from Pedro de Ribadeneyra, *Hystoria Ecclesiastica del Scisma del Reino de Inglaterra* [The ecclesiastical history of the schism of the realm of England] (Lisbon, 1589). Greenlee 4552 .R616 1589. Newberry Library, Chicago.

FIGURE 75. Christopher Saxton, proof sheet of "Northumberland," annotated by William Cecil, Lord Burghley, 1575. MS Royal 18 D. III, fols. 71v–72r. Reproduced by permission of the British Library.

On July 19 the Spanish were sighted off the coast of Cornwall, in southwest England. For the next eight days, the English fleet dogged the Spanish along the south coast of England, alternately engaging and maneuvering, always pushing the Spanish away from the shore. By July 28 the Spanish fleet was at Calais. That midnight, the English sent unmanned fireships into the midst of the Spanish fleet and scattered them. July 29 saw a desperate battle, with the Spanish pounded on one side by the English fleet and threatened on the other by the coastal shoals. Then the wind shifted and the Spanish ran into the North Sea. What would happen now? Would they wheel south again to attack? Would Parma attempt to bring his army across the Channel on his own?

When the Spanish had swung around the southeast coast toward the mouth of the Thames, the approaches to London had been carefully fortified (figure 76). The map by Robert Adams shows the reach of the shore batteries at regular intervals, arrayed to stop a fleet coming up the river to the capital. Adams's map also charts Elizabeth's own principal role in rallying her people. On August 7, as the English still waited to see if the Spanish would reappear, Elizabeth set out from her palace at Greenwich. She traveled overland to St. James, and then on August 8 came down the Thames by barge to Tilbury, where her army lay in readiness. The next day she delivered her most famous speech, which became central to her legend.

What exactly Elizabeth said that day we can never know. Multiple versions exist, each reported by someone who claimed to have heard it. We may assume that the speech underwent the normal process: carefully prepared by Elizabeth and her chief ministers, delivered from memory as if it were spontaneous—and no doubt with improvisations— written down by those in the audience, and then carefully improved and circulated. The best-known version may not be the most accurate, but it is certainly the version that Elizabeth herself wanted her people to remember (figure 77):

> My loving people: I have been persuaded by some, that are careful of my safety, to take heed how I committed my self to armed multitudes for fear of treachery. But I tell you, that I would not desire to live to distrust my faithful and loving people. Let tyrants fear. I have so behaved my self, that under god I have placed my chiefest strength and safeguard in the loyal hearts and goodwill of my subjects. Wherefore I am come among you at this time, [not] for my recreation and pleasure, [but] being resolved in the midst and heat of the battle to live and die amongst you all, to lay down for my god, and for my kingdom and for my people mine honor and my blood run in the dust. I know I have the body but of a weak and feeble woman, but I have the heart and stomach of a king, and of a king of England too, and take foul scorn that Parma or any prince of Europe should dare to invade the borders of my realm.
>
> To the which rather than any dishonor shall grow by me, I myself will venture my blood, myself will be your general, judge and rewarder of your virtue in the field. I know that already for your forwardness you have deserved rewards and crowns and I assure

FIGURE 76. Robert Adams, "Thamesis Descriptio," 1588. MS Additional 44839. Reproduced by permission of the British Library.

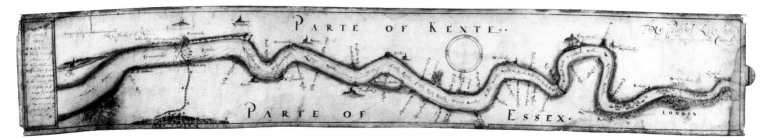

My louinge people, I haue bin perswaded by
om, y.t ar carefull of my saffty, to take heed
how I committed my selfe to armed multi-
tudz for fear of treachery. Butt I tell you
that I would not desire to liue to distrust
my faythfull and louing people. Letty ty-
rantz fear: but I haue so behaued my
selfe, y.t vnder god I haue placed my
chiefest strength and safgard in y.e loyall
hartz and goodwill of my subiectz. wher.
for I am com amoungst you att this butt for
my recreation and pleasure, being resolued
in y.e middst, and heate of y.e battle to
liue and dye amoungst you all, to lay
down for my god, and for my kingdom, and for my people myn honor
and my blood euen in y.e dust. I know
I haue y.e body butt of a weake and feble
woman, butt I haue y.e harte and sto=
mak of a kinge, and of a kynge of
england too. and take foule scorn y.t par=
ma or any prince of Europe should dare
to inuade y.e borders of my realm:

Virginia

The European discovery and conquest of America provides historical bookends for the life of Elizabeth. When Columbus set out from Spain in 1492, Elizabeth's grandfather Henry VII was on the throne of England. Her father's first wife, Katharine of Aragon, was the daughter of Columbus's patron Isabella of Castile. In 1585, Sir Walter Raleigh established the Virginia Colony at Roanoke Island (now North Carolina). The first successful English colony, at Jamestown, was established in 1607, just four years after Elizabeth's death, by the Virginia Company, and named for Elizabeth's successor, James I.

Even as the colonies were created, many Europeans were fascinated with the appearance, cultures, and lands of the indigenous peoples. They marveled at the well-ordered villages (figure 78), reminiscent of those in rural England. They relished reports of unfamiliar religious practices, and enticing foods and herbs, including tobacco.

Elizabeth's own interest in America probably had little to do with colonies or exotic cultures. To her, America was a huge strategic asset for Spain, supplying it with gold and silver to finance its military might. And it was Spain's soft underbelly, with a long, thinly defended coastline and even longer transatlantic supply lines vulnerable to her skilled sea captains, including Sir John Hawkins, Sir Richard Grenville, and above all, Sir Francis Drake.

To Elizabeth's chief ministers and to the commercial leaders of London, America was a vast opportunity for making money. There were numerous schemes for the "plantation" of America, especially of the Atlantic seaboard to the north of the Spanish colonies. English investors (with the direct or covert involvement of Elizabeth herself) would establish colonies of English settlers that could trade directly with the Spanish, or send back their own commodities of sugar, ginger, and tobacco. And, by no coincidence, the colonies would make excellent bases for raids on Spanish shipping by "privateers"—essentially pirates, operating with the blessing of the queen. The plantation venture began in earnest with Raleigh's 1585 colony at Roanoke Island, with the grudging assistance of its Algonquin inhabitants (figure 79).

The convergence of strategic and economic motives is illustrated by Drake's expedition in 1585–86 to America (plate 9). Setting out from Plymouth to relieve English shipping threatened by the Spanish, he then swung south and west and crossed the Atlantic. On New Years Day 1586, he staged a daring land-and-sea attack, destroying the great Spanish fortress at Santo Domingo. This was followed by a lightning raid on Cartagena, on the South American mainland, before he swung north again. Running up the Florida coast, he plundered St. Augustine, and then sailed on to relieve the colonists at Roanoke. "Virginia" was at an end until after Elizabeth and Drake were both dead, but shortly after, the colony would be renewed a few miles to the north at Jamestown.

FIGURE 78. "The Towne of Secota," from Thomas Hariot, *A briefe and true report of the new found land of Virginia* (Frankfurt, 1590). Ayer *f150.5 V7 H2 1590, plate 20. Newberry Library, Chicago.

The arriual of the Englishemen in Virginia. II.

FIGURE 79. "The arrival of the Englishemen in Virginia," from Thomas Hariot, *A briefe and true report of the new found land of Virginia* (Frankfurt, 1590). Ayer *f150.5 V7 H2 1590, plate 2. Newberry Library, Chicago.

you in the word of a prince you shall not fail of them. In the mean time my Lieutenant General [the earl of Leicester] shall be in my stead, than whom never prince commanded a more noble or worthy subject. Not doubting but by your concord in the camp and valor in the field and your obedience to my self and my general, we shall shortly have a famous victory over this enemy of my god and of my kingdom.[54]

The speech has all of her hallmarks, including the claim to rule by love, and the sense of closeness to God and her people. Above all, it shows how she could, in the words of the Scottish ambassador years earlier, be both king and queen at once.

Elizabeth did not of course stay on the battlefield to shed her blood, as she promised in the beginning of her speech. Instead, she left the battlefield to her generals, as she said she would at the conclusion. But the irony is that, unbeknownst to her or her troops, the victory was already won. The Spanish fleet was more damaged than even Drake realized. It was too far north to link up with Parma's army in the Netherlands. Instead, it faced a perilous journey farther north, then west and south again around Scotland and Ireland in order to get back to Spain. Only a fraction would make it.

If the English weren't at first sure they had won, the Spanish at first didn't realize they had lost. Throughout August 1588 and into September, pamphlets circulated proclaiming a great Spanish victory—some based more on expectations than on actual reports. They claimed that the Spanish army had landed and marched to London. Drake and the other leaders were killed or captured. Elizabeth herself had abandoned her capital and was in the field with the army, but faced a mutiny from English Catholics. The end, they claimed, was near. The English pamphlets in answer were hysterical, but more accurate. *A Packe of Spanish Lyes . . . Now ripped up, unfolded, and . . . worthy to be damned and burned* prints English and Spanish versions in parallel columns, with bold letters to show where the Spanish claims were most false (figure 80).

But even as the English started to celebrate their victory, they feared another invasion with the next season. It took a half dozen years for the fears to subside, and fifteen years to sign a treaty of peace—by which time Philip and Elizabeth were both dead and gone. In the interim the defeat of the Armada became the subject of its own legend. Elizabeth's speech at Tilbury was circulated in manuscript reports and in print. The commanders were lauded, and the admiral, Charles Lord Howard of Effingham, commissioned great tapestries, which later were hung in the House of Lords, showing the sea-battles day by day. The tapestries themselves were destroyed when Parliament burned in 1834, but eighteenth-century engravings of them show how thoroughly the event informed the national consciousness (figure 81). By then, England had supplanted Spain as the world's dominant power, and many traced the change, however inaccurately, to the triumph of Elizabeth.

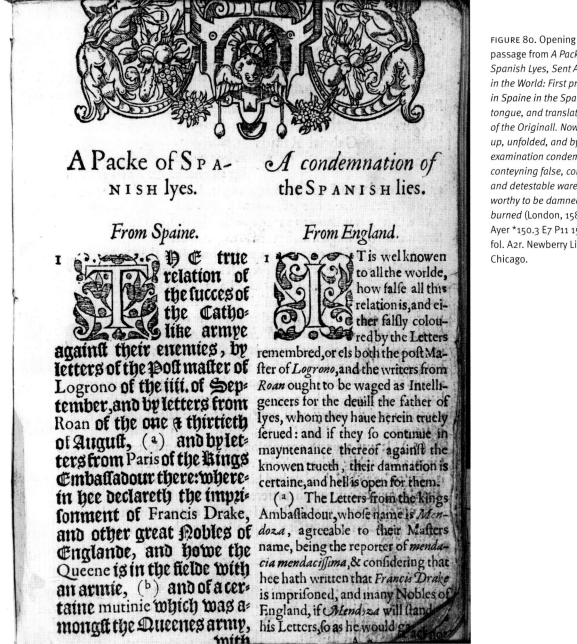

A Packe of Spa-nish lyes.

From Spaine.

1 THe true relation of the succes of the Catho-like armye against their enemies, by letters of the Post master of Logrono of the iiii. of Sep-tember, and by letters from Roan of the one & thirtieth of August, (a) and by let-ters from Paris of the Kings Embassadour there: where-in hee declareth the impri-sonment of Francis Drake, and other great Nobles of Englande, and howe the Queene is in the fielde with an armie, (b) and of a cer-taine mutinie which was a-mongst the Queenes army, with

A condemnation of the Spanish lies.

From England.

1 IT is wel knowen to all the worlde, how false all this relation is, and ei-ther falsly colou-red by the Letters remembred, or els both the post Ma-ster of Logrono, and the writers from Roan ought to be waged as Intelli-gencers for the deuill the father of lyes, whom they haue herein truely serued: and if they so continue in mayntenance thereof against the knowen trueth, their damnation is certaine, and hell is open for them.

(a) The Letters from the kings Ambassadour, whose name is Men-doza, agreeable to their Masters name, being the reporter of menda-cia mendacissima, & considering that hee hath written that Francis Drake is imprisoned, and many Nobles of England, if Mendoza will stand his Letters, so as he would gather

FIGURE 80. Opening passage from *A Packe of Spanish Lyes, Sent Abroad in the World: First printed in Spaine in the Spanish tongue, and translated out of the Originall. Now ripped up, unfolded, and by just examination condemned, as conteyning false, corrupt, and detestable wares, worthy to be damned and burned* (London, 1588). Ayer *150.3 E7 P11 1588, fol. A2r. Newberry Library, Chicago.

FIGURE 81. John Pine, after Cornelius Vroom, "The Spanish and English Fleets off the Isle of Portland," from *The Engravings of the Hangings of the House of Lords* (London, 1739). Case Y 008 .76, plate 5. Newberry Library, Chicago.

England and the Idea of Empire

The Tudor monarch was sometimes called an "imperial crown." Originally this meant simply that the king of England did not owe feudal allegiance to any greater earthly power and considered himself to be on an equal footing with the Holy Roman Emperor. (This became especially important once Henry VIII had broken with Rome and found himself in conflict with the emperor.) But gradually the idea took on its modern meaning, that the English monarch ruled not only the English, but distant lands and peoples.

Both ideas are captured in the title that Elizabeth herself usually went by, which was "Queen of England, France, and Ireland." After 1586, "Virginia" is added to the list. The claim to France was simply a gesture toward the medieval past, since England had lost its last French possessions under Elizabeth's sister, Mary. Her title to Virginia was empty after the small band of settlers on Roanoke had been abandoned to their fate. But most troubled and troubling was Elizabeth's claim to rule over Ireland.

A series of English kings, including Henry VIII, had tried to control Ireland by having its feudal lords swear obedience. The Irish aristocracy had family ties to the English aristocracy, and Elizabeth counted a number of the Irish lords among her cousins. But for most of the Irish, this loose alliance, full of compromise, was unacceptable, since the English differed from them in language, in culture, and—after Henry's reformation—in religion. It was unacceptable to the Spanish, who tried repeatedly to establish a beachhead in Ireland. And it was also unacceptable to English settlers, who lived on lands confiscated from those who had revolted against Elizabeth. Prominent among them was the poet Edmund Spenser, who pros-

pered as an English governmental official in Ireland and wrote his finest poetry there, until his estate was burned in a rebellion in 1598.

A succession of Elizabethan governors tried to subdue the island, including Sir Henry Sidney (father of the poet Philip Sidney) and the first earl of Essex (father of the more famous Essex whose own attempt to conquer Ireland was a disaster). English control was weakest in the interior of the island and along its west coast, and strongest in an area of the northeast, known as the Pale (figure 82). What lay past that region was, for the English, literally "beyond the Pale"—the meaning being much the same now as it was then. The current division of the island between the Republic of Ireland and Northern Ireland roughly reflects this ancient division.

If Ireland whetted the appetite of the English monarchy to rule over other cultures, it was Sir Francis Drake's voyage around the world that ignited a national dream of empire. Drake set out in 1577 on a voyage of piracy among the Spanish ships in the Caribbean. Since it was too dangerous to go back the way he had come, he followed Magellan's lead and went south and west around South America, still plundering the Spanish as he ran up the Pacific coast. He perhaps got well north of San Francisco Bay, and claimed the region for Elizabeth under the name of New Albion.

Then Drake struck across the Pacific, circled Africa, and arrived back in England three years after he had left. The voyage was not only heroic but also immensely profitable, both for Drake himself and for his queen. His feat was celebrated in books and a notable map, in which the line of his route circles the globe. At bottom center is his ship, the *Golden Hind,* and inset pictures in the corners depict his chief exploits (figure 83). (A smudge on the map along the California coast shows the cartographer's response to conflicting reports over just how far north Drake got.)

In the eighteenth and nineteenth centuries, English imperial power, based on its navy, would indeed circle the globe, reaching its zenith under another queen, Victoria. Elizabeth protected Drake, knighted him, and shared in his profits, but it is hard to believe that she could have imagined what he was setting in motion.

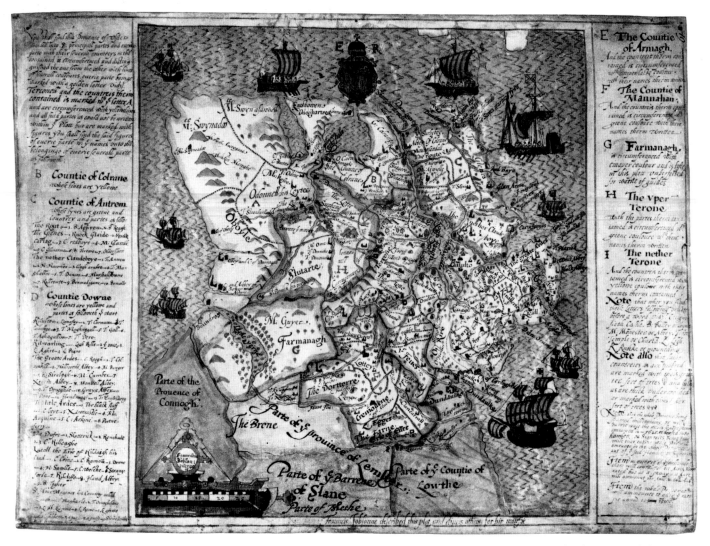

FIGURE 82. Francis Jobson, map of Ulster, circa 1590. MS Cotton Augustus I. ii. 19. Reproduced by permission of the British Library.

ELIZABETH I

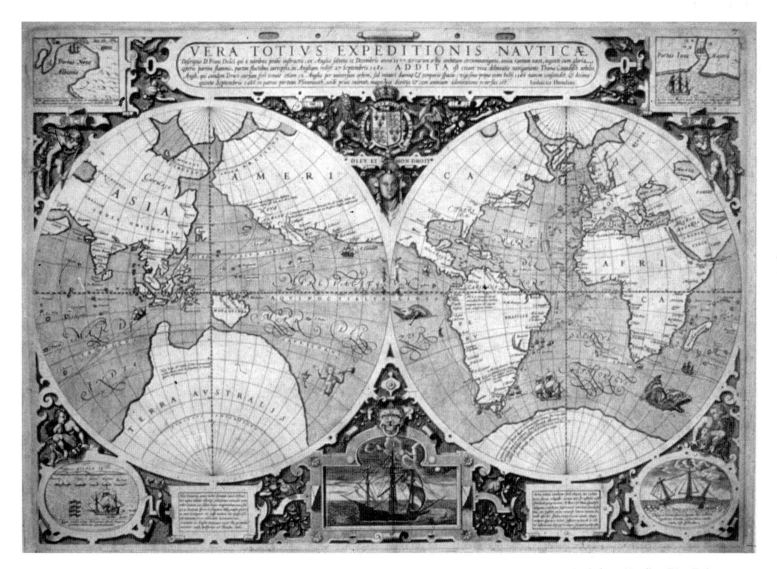

FIGURE 83. Jodocus Hondius, "Vera Totius
Expeditionis Nauticae" [An accurate description
of the voyage around the world of Sir Francis
Drake], circa 1595. Engraving, 38.5 × 54.5 cm.
Arthur Holzheimer Collection.

DEATH
AND AFTER

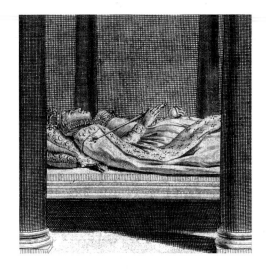

The interval from the first sighting of the Armada off Cornwall through the great speech at Tilbury was a mere three weeks. But the accomplishments of that perilously brief moment guaranteed the fame of Elizabeth. Thirty years after ascending the throne, she was at last secure and safe. She was Gloriana, having won a victory that had not been seen since Agincourt and would not be seen again until Waterloo. She had stirred the patriotism of her people in defense of their island as none would do until Winston Churchill. But the victory of the Armada also, in a strange and ironic way, guaranteed her irrelevancy.

There was, in short, nowhere to go but down. The peace brought an explosion of creativity for the nation. The comedies and histories of Shakespeare, the mature poetry of Edmund Spenser, the early verse of Ben Jonson and John Donne, were primarily products of the 1590s. But as the nation turned its energies to the pursuits of peace, it began to look beyond the aging queen. By the mid-1590s—as Shakespeare was at work on *Romeo and Juliet*, *A Midsummer Night's Dream*, and *Henry IV*—Elizabeth was past sixty and had outlived her old supporters, Leicester and Walsingham. Burghley was near death. Those younger were thinking about what would come next, and preparing to serve King James.

Besides, the formal conflict with Spain dragged on. There were occasional raids and threats on both sides, without serious war, and without the benefits of peace. England was a nation whose prosperity depended on trade, and the lack of a resolution to

Elizabeth and the Poets

The last twenty years of Elizabeth's reign was a golden era for English poetry, producing such masterpieces as Edmund Spenser's *Faerie Queene* and the sonnets of William Shakespeare and Sir Philip Sidney. Elizabeth herself was frequently a subject for the poets, and they contributed greatly to her legend.

When Elizabeth came to the throne, the English could boast of the achievements of Geoffrey Chaucer in his native tongue, but Latin was still the language of international literary prestige. William Alabaster embarked on a Latin epic poem in praise of Elizabeth, called "Elisæis" (figure 84). In the rare surviving manuscripts of the poem, the

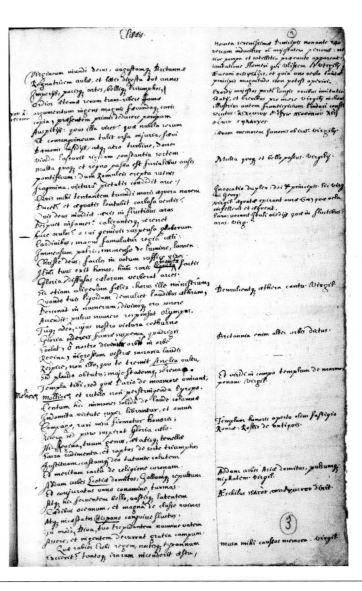

FIGURE 84. William Alabaster, "Elisæis," circa 1591. Case MS Y.682 .A3, fol. 3r. Newberry Library, Chicago.

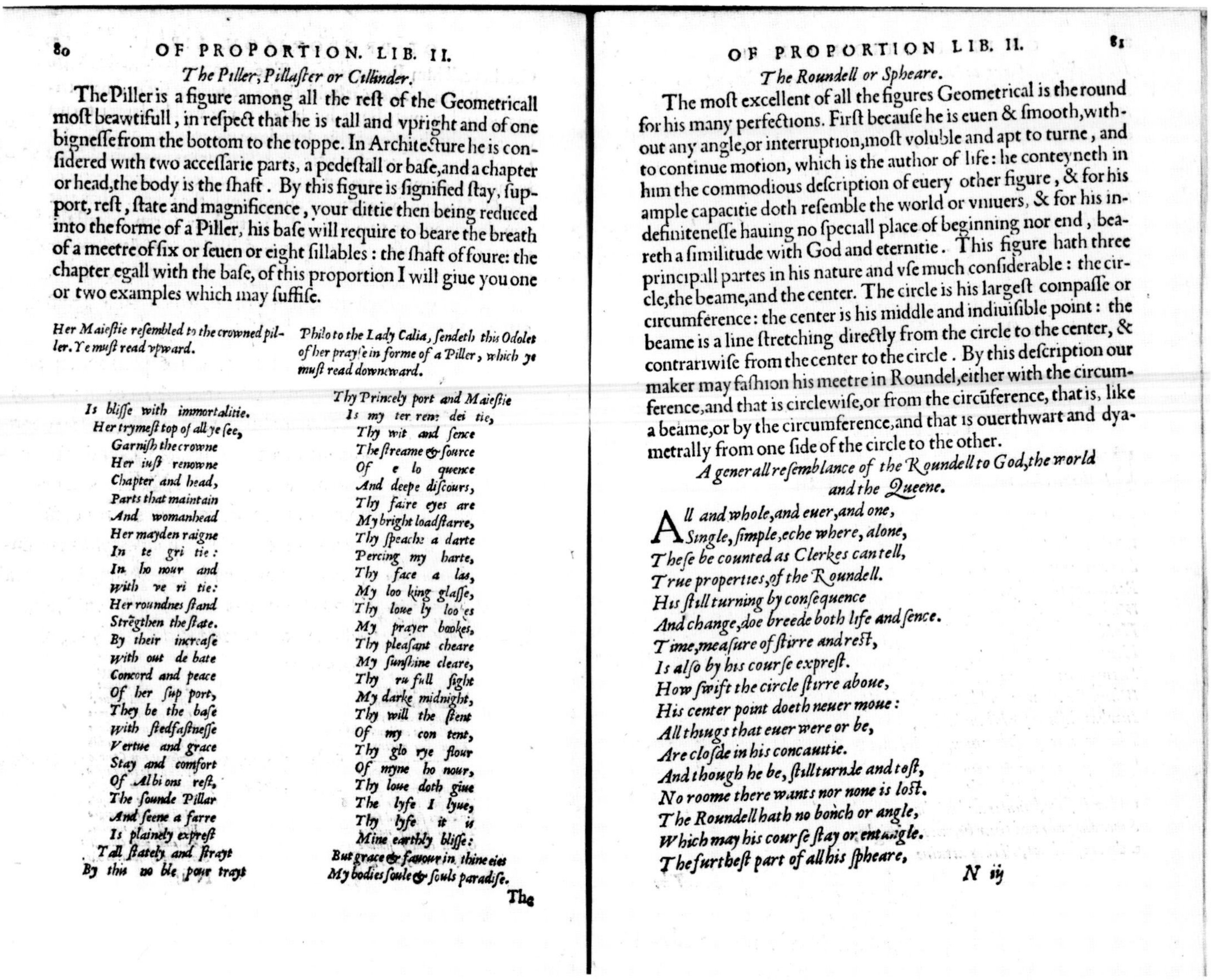

The Piller, Pillaster or Cillinder.

The Piller is a figure among all the rest of the Geometricall most beawtifull, in respect that he is tall and vpright and of one bignesse from the bottom to the toppe. In Architecture he is considered with two accessarie parts, a pedestall or base, and a chapter or head, the body is the shaft. By this figure is signified stay, support, rest, state and magnificence, your dittie then being reduced into the forme of a Piller, his base will require to beare the breath of a meetre of six or seuen or eight sillables: the shaft of foure: the chapter egall with the base, of this proportion I will giue you one or two examples which may suffise.

Her Maiestie resembled to the crowned piller. Ye must read vpward.

Is blisse with immortalitie.
Her trymest top of all ye see,
Garnish the crowne
Her iust renowne
Chapter and head,
Parts that maintain
And womanhead
Her mayden raigne
In te gri tie:
In ho nour and
with ve ri tie:
Her roundnes stand
Strēgthen the state.
By their increase
with out de bate
Concord and peace
Of her sup port,
They be the base
with stedfastnesse
Vertue and grace
Stay and comfort
Of Albions rest,
The sounde Pillar
And seene a farre
Is plainely exprest
Tall stately and strayt
By this no ble pour trayt

Philo to the Lady Calia, sendeth this Odolet of her prayse in forme of a Piller, which ye must read downeward.

Thy Princely port and Maiestie
Is my ter rem dei tic,
Thy wit and sence
The streame & source
Of e lo quence
And deepe discours,
Thy faire eyes are
My bright loadstarre,
Thy speach a darte
Percing my harte,
Thy face a las,
My loo king glasse,
Thy loue ly loo es
My prayer bookes,
Thy pleasant cheare
My sunshine cleare,
Thy ru full sight
My darke midnight,
Thy will the stent
Of my con tent,
Thy glo rye flour
Of myne ho nour,
Thy loue doth giue
The lyfe I lyue,
Thy lyfe it is
Mine earthly blisse:
But grace & fauour in thine eies
My bodies soule & souls paradise.

The

The Roundell or Spheare.

The most excellent of all the figures Geometrical is the round for his many perfections. First because he is euen & smooth, without any angle, or interruption, most voluble and apt to turne, and to continue motion, which is the author of life: he conteyneth in him the commodious description of euery other figure, & for his ample capacitie doth resemble the world or vniuers, & for his indefinitenesse hauing no speciall place of beginning nor end, beareth a similitude with God and eternitie. This figure hath three principall partes in his nature and vse much considerable: the circle, the beame, and the center. The circle is his largest compasse or circumference: the center is his middle and indiuisible point: the beame is a line stretching directly from the circle to the center, & contrariwise from the center to the circle. By this description our maker may fashion his meetre in Roundel, either with the circumference, and that is circlewise, or from the circuference, that is, like a beame, or by the circumference, and that is ouerthwart and dyametrally from one side of the circle to the other.

A generall resemblance of the Roundell to God, the world and the Queene.

All and whole, and euer, and one,
Single, simple, eche where, alone,
These be counted as Clerkes can tell,
True properties, of the Roundell.
His still turning by consequence
And change, doe breede both life and sence.
Time, measure of stirre and rest,
Is also by his course exprest.
How swift the circle stirre aboue,
His center point doeth neuer moue:
All things that euer were or be,
Are closde in his concauitie.
And though he be, still turnde and tost,
No roome there wants nor none is lost.
The Roundell hath no bouch or angle,
Which may his course stay or entangle.
The furthest part of all his spheare,

N iij

FIGURE 85. "Shaped verses" on Elizabeth I, from [George Puttenham], *The Arte of English Poesie* (London, 1589). Case YO4 .719, fols. N2v–N3r. Newberry Library, Chicago.

left column contains Alabaster's verses, while the right lists parallels to the great Latin epic the *Aeneid,* written by the poet Virgil in the first century B.C.E. to honor Augustus Caesar. Alabaster's work did not find favor, however, and he left it incomplete.

By contrast, George Puttenham set out to explain the principles of poetry in English by writing verse directly in praise of Elizabeth. He was particularly interested in shaped poems. For instance, a poem listing the personal perfections of Elizabeth could be shaped like a pillar, which itself signified magnificence (figure 85).

The greatest triumph of Elizabethan poetry is Spenser's *Faerie Queene* (figure 86). A monumental work in six books, the poem weaves together Arthurian legend with classical models to create a "glorious pourtraict" of Elizabeth's "fayrest vertue, far above the rest."[1] The poem established English as an epic language rivaling Latin, and it had no rivals in the language until John Milton wrote *Paradise Lost* nearly eighty years later.

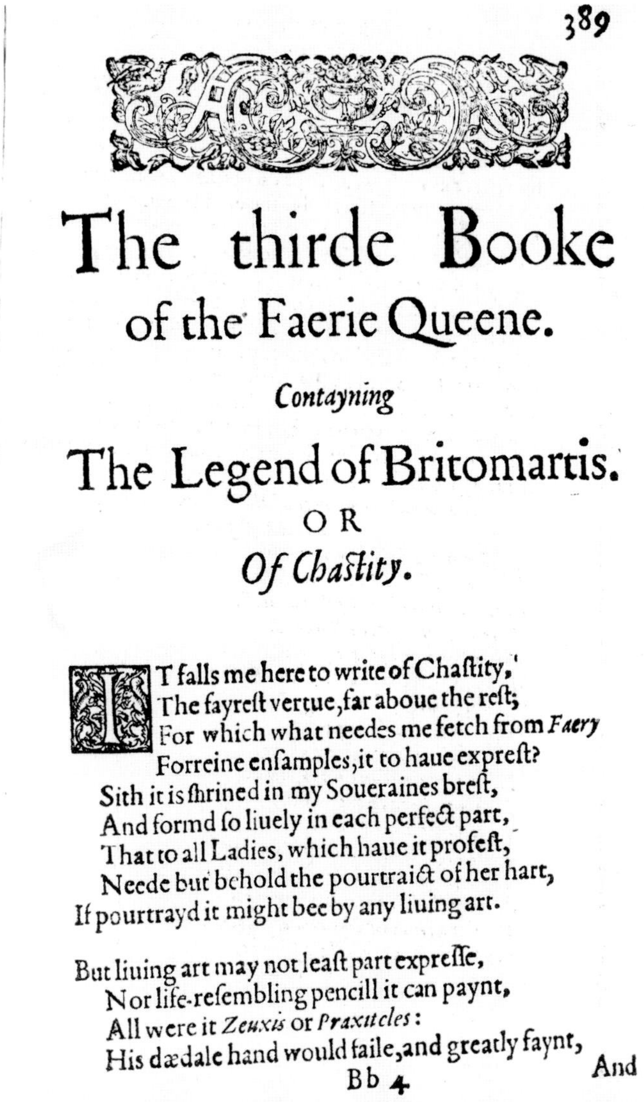

NOTE

1. Edmund Spenser, *The Faerie Queene* (London, 1590), 3.Proem.1–3.

389

The thirde Booke
of the Faerie Queene.

Contayning

The Legend of Britomartis.
OR
Of Chastity.

T falls me here to write of Chastity,
  The fayrest vertue, far aboue the rest;
  For which what needes me fetch from *Faery*
  Forreine enfamples, it to haue exprest?
Sith it is shrined in my Soueraines brest,
And formd so liuely in each perfect part,
That to all Ladies, which haue it profest,
Neede but behold the pourtraict of her hart,
If pourtrayd it might bee by any liuing art.

But liuing art may not least part expresse,
  Nor life-resembling pencill it can paynt,
  All were it *Zeuxis* or *Praxiteles*:
  His dædale hand would faile, and greatly faynt,
         Bb 4   And

FIGURE 86. Proem to Book III, from Edmund Spenser, *The Faerie Queene* (London, 1590). Case 4A .923, vol. 1, p. 389. Newberry Library, Chicago.

the old conflict meant the disruption of its commerce with both Northern Europe and the Mediterranean.

Elizabeth herself was preparing James for the throne of England. She never quite acknowledged him as her heir, but once they had gotten past the matter of his mother's death, she treated him as if he were. She called herself a loving mother and sister to him, and sent him regular letters of advice on the craft of monarchy. Characteristic is one she wrote in January 1593 (figure 87). She claims to have watched over James since his birth, to have fought Philip of Spain and the Armada in order to protect him, at cost of "the blood of many of my dear subjects' lives."[55] (In effect she is asking, if the Spanish had won, what would there be for him to inherit?) She gives him hints—they sound more like demands—for the handling of the latest Spanish conspiracies. She then apologizes for "my too long scribbling," and signs herself "Your loving, affectionate sister, Elizabeth R."[56]

James in turn made clear his acceptance of the bargain and his readiness, answering her with an equal mix of frankness and statecraft, and in letters written with his own hand. He named his first daughter Elizabeth in 1596 and invested her in the symbolism of her namesake. Her childhood calligraphy book, made after her father was on the throne of England, was designed to teach her ethics, good handwriting, and the French language (figure 88). The book is evidence that she received, at least in part, an education like that bestowed on Elizabeth herself and her mother, Anne Boleyn. She is addressed in words that almost would have suited Elizabeth the Queen: "Madame Elizabeth, file vnique du Roy de la grand Bretagne . . . un Phoenix de vostre age"—"Madam Elizabeth, unique daughter of the king of Great Britain, . . . a phoenix of our age."[57]

So death did not come too soon to Elizabeth, at least if the legend was to live on. When the time came at last in March 1603, the nation was well prepared. Poets wrote elegies for Elizabeth, some good, some bad. One Thomas Newton, for instance, rushed into print with *Atropoïon Delion, Or, The death of Delia: With the Teares of her funerall. A Pöeticall Excusive Discourse of our late Eliza* (figure 89). Under the running head "Eliza's Funerall," he immortalized his queen in this fashion:

> Our eyes did now behold their last beholding
> Of Delia's shape, wrapped in obscurity
> Till that the crummy Earth her corpse enfolding
> Had blinded us with his condensity
> Returning then our thoughts began to paint
> Her lively shape with new rememberance.[58]

The English merchant Thomas Smith describes how he carried the news of her death to Tsar Boris Godunov in far-off Russia. "Striking his hand advisedly on his breast, 'Oh,'

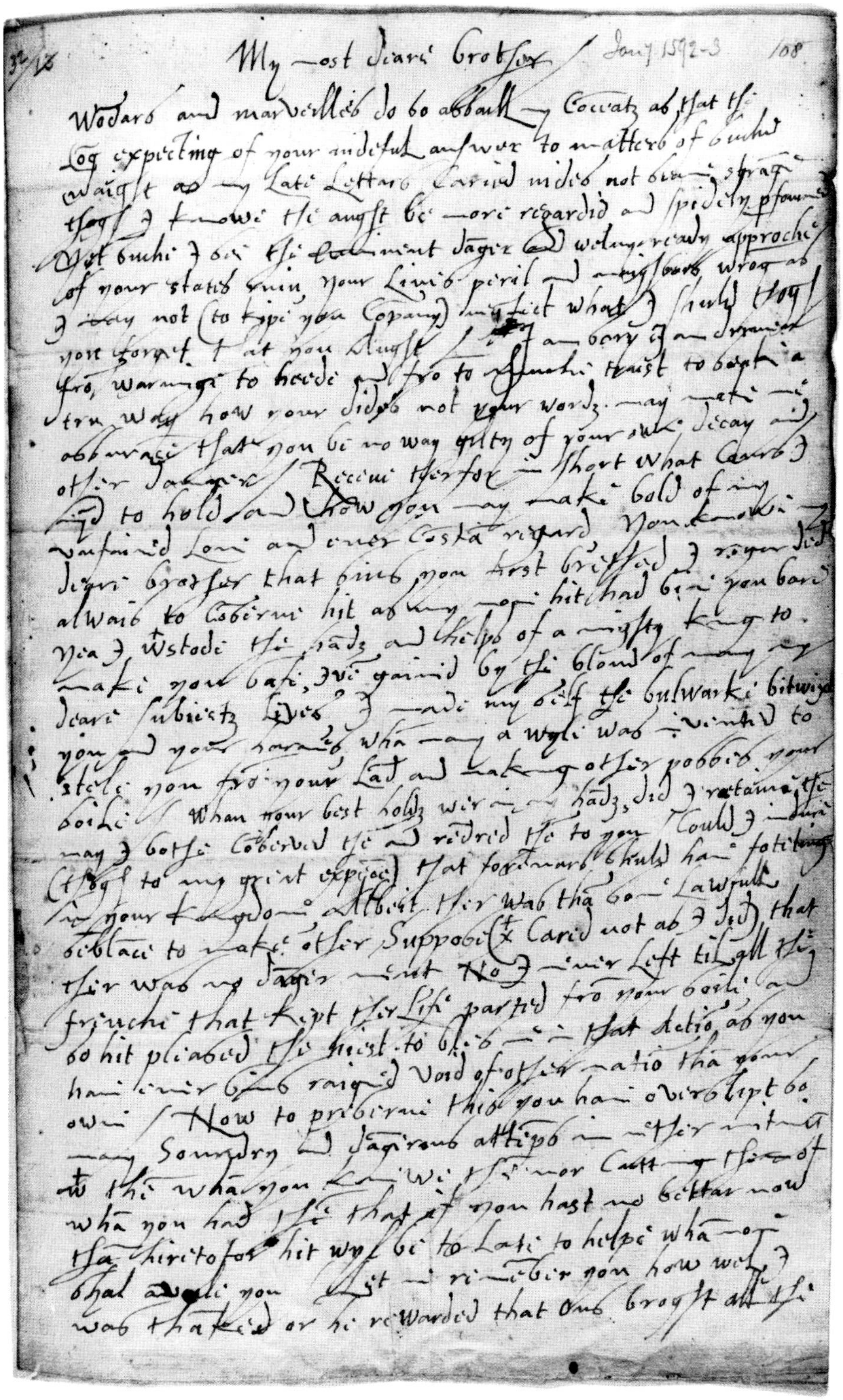

32/18 My most deare brother / Jany 1592-3 108

Wondars and marvells do so assail my Conceats as that the
long expecting of your nedeful answer to matters of such
waight as my late letters caried makes me not a litle strange
thogh I knowe the aught be more regarded and spedely performed
but such I see the lamentable danger and welnere ready approches
of your states ruin, your lives peril and neighbors wrong as
I may not (to kepe you company) neglect what I shuld (thogh
you forget) that at you aught ...

FIGURE 87. Elizabeth I, letter to James VI of Scotland, January 1593. MS Additional 23240, art. 32, fol. 108r. Reproduced by permission of the British Library.

A Madame Elizabeth, fille vnique du
Roy de la grand Bretaigne.

L'honneur qui se doit rendre aux merites des grands
Donnent mille proiects a vn gentil courage,
Pour se manifester par vn beau tesmoignage,
De ce qu'il a compris dans les arts florissans.
Le zele que ie dois aux effects paroissans
Des vertus qui vous font vn Phœnix de vostre aage,
Me pousse a vous offrir ce mien petit ouurage,
Tesmoin de l'exercice ou i'ay passé mes ans.
Receuez d'vn bon œil PRINCESSE, ie vous prie,
L'ouurage & l'ouurier de qui le cœur n'oublie
Les tres-humbles respects qui par luy vous son deus:
A vous donc il consacre & sa main & sa plume
Sans la plume les noms des Princes ne sont leus,
Et le temps rauissant dans l'oubly les consume.

FIGURE 88. Dedication from Jean de Beauchesne, "A Madame Elizabeth, fille unique du Roy de la grand Bretaigne" [Calligraphy book for Princess Elizabeth Stuart], circa 1610. Wing MS ZW 639 .B382. Newberry Library, Chicago.

said he, 'my dear Sister Queen Elizabeth, whom I loved as mine own heart,' expressing this his great affection almost in a weeping passion."[59]

For others it was, in the words of Shakespeare's Claudius, a time of "defeated joy . . . in equal scale weighing delight and dole." Grief for the old queen mingled with celebrations of the new king (figure 90). The Scottish king's triumphal entry into London and coronation were heralded in pamphlets in England and abroad (figure 91). Ben Jonson helped to design the pageantry, and William Shakespeare—as a member of the theater company of the King's Men—marched in the coronation procession.

Meanwhile, the obsequies for the dead queen had to be observed. Elizabeth's funeral cortege is recorded in two manuscripts, one an album of colored drawings, the other a magnificent scroll, over forty feet in length, showing in careful pen-and-ink renderings each participant in his or her proper order (figures 94–97). The procession

HEROES.

OVr eyes did now behold their laſt beholding
  Of *Delias* ſhape, wrapt in obſcuritie:
Till that the crummie Earth her corpes infoulding,
  Had blinded vs with his condenſitie :
Returning then our thoughtes, began to paint
  Her lyuelie ſhape with new rememberaunce :
And comming to her face, a new Complaint
  Grew, thinking on ſo ſweete a countenaunce, |
That then we thought we had a new to make
  Both mourning veſtmentes, teares, graue, hearſe and all:
For *Delia* ſeem'd a new in life to wake,
  When was but done a new her Funerall.
    A griefe vnto vs all, to them moſt wretched,
    To whom our *Deliaes* loue and bountie ſtretched.

FIGURE 89. "Heroes."
A verse of lament on the death of Elizabeth I, from Thomas Newton, *Atropoïon Delion, Or, The death of Delia: With the Teares of her Funerall. A Pöeticall Excusive Discourse of our late Eliza* (London, 1603). Case 4A .911, fol. B2v. Newberry Library, Chicago.

FIGURE 90. Nicholas Hilliard, *James I,* circa 1610. Ink and color on vellum, diameter 4.5 cm. Mr. and Mrs. John H. Bryan.

DISCOVRS TRIOMPHAL.

CONTENANT EN

BREF L'ARRIVEMENT EN AN-
GLETERRE DE TRESCHER ET SOV-
uerain seigneur, le Roy Iacques, son couron-
nement à Vvestmunster. Ensemble son entree
royalle à Londres commençant depuis son
chasteau de la Tour, iusques a son mannoir
Royal de Vvithal-

*Remonstrans aussi les raretez, & varietez des trophees & thea-
tres dressees, tant par les valeureux citoyens de ceste honorable ville de Londres, que par les autres nations, comme Ita-
liens, François, & Flamés, auec declaration de la venue
du Roy, & de la Royne sur leschange de Londres.
Fait par Gilbert Dugdale.*

Imprimé à Londres par R. B. 1604.

A ROVEN,

Traduict d'Anglois en François, & imprimé par
IEAN PETIT, tenant sa boutique en
la cour du Palais.

1604.

The Queen and the Theater

At the conclusion of the film *Shakespeare in Love,* Queen Elizabeth goes to a performance at the Curtain playhouse, only to declare that "the Queen of England does not attend exhibitions of public lewdness so something is out of joint."[1] She was, as always, entirely correct. For Elizabeth did not go to the theater. The Elizabethan theater came to her. The Curtain, like the Rose and Shakespeare's Globe, was in the wrong part of town, amidst the bear-baiting ring and the houses of prostitution, and distant from the splendor of the palaces at Greenwich, Whitehall, and Hampton Court (figure 92).

The dramatic achievements of William Shakespeare and Ben Jonson have their beginnings in the reign of Elizabeth I, and the short, brilliant, and bizarre career of Christopher Marlowe falls entirely within her time on the throne. This is not a coincidence. For Elizabeth's lord chamberlain, who was responsible for generating entertainment for the queen during holidays and court revels, also supervised the Master of the Revels, whose job it was to regulate, license, and

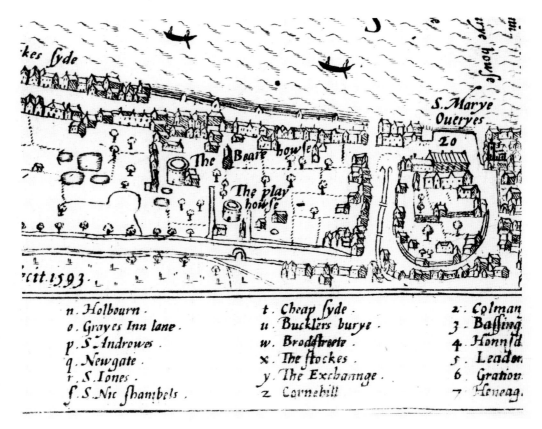

FIGURE 92. "The play howse." Detail of "London," from John Norden, *Speculum Britanniae* (London, 1593). Case G45004 .6, after fol. 36. Newberry Library, Chicago.

A
PLEASANT
Conceited Comedie
CALLED,
Loues labors loſt.

As it vvas preſented before her Highnes
this laſt Chriſtmas.

Newly corrected and augmented
By W. Shakeſpere.

Imprinted at London by W.W.
for Cutbert Burby.
1598.

FIGURE 93. Title page from William Shakespeare, *A Pleasant Conceited Comedie Called, Loves labors lost* (London, 1598). Case 4A .949. Newberry Library, Chicago.

censor the commercial theaters in which all Elizabethan playwrights worked.

The process is visible on the title page of the first printing of Shakespeare's play *A Pleasant Conceited Comedie Called, Loves labors lost* (figure 93). This comedy was "presented before her Highness this last Christmas" (probably for the revels on Twelfth Night, or January 5—the "twelfth day of Christmas"). It is not only "pleasant" but also "conceited," meaning it is full of concepts, and hence fit entertainment for the monarch and her court. Shakespeare gets second billing as an "augmentor" or "corrector" of the play, but clearly, in the mind of the bookseller, Cuthbert Burby, the queen's interest is what authorizes our own.

Although royal pageants and interludes had been enjoyed by English monarchs for centuries, it was Elizabeth's government that established a stable structure for regular productions at court. This was a costly enterprise, requiring not only craftsmen and materials, but also the best actors and playwrights. In 1574, the Earl of Leicester's Men became the first playing company to receive a patent, allowing them to set up business on the outskirts of London. A thriving theater market quickly grew up, with as many as ten commercial playhouses in operation by 1600. Out of this theater market came talented players, elaborate costumes, and occasionally suitable scripts from which the Master of the Revels could obtain, with less expense, dramatic entertainments for the queen. The Office of the Revels, in other words, helped to create the economic and institutional conditions that made it possible for playwrights, actors, and theater managers to make a living.

Many of these theaters—such as the Globe, the Rose, and the Swan—were positioned just outside the jurisdiction of London city officials. If the theaters were popular with the court, they were sometimes the targets both of religious zealots and of business owners whose wives and workers spent their money and time at the playhouses. But the theaters around London continued to prosper, at least until they were closed in 1642 by the revolutionary Oliver Cromwell. While the golden age of English Renaissance theater had come to an end, its present health and influence can surely be measured by the thousands of performances, books, and films that Elizabethan dramatists still inspire every year.

—Jonathan Walker

NOTE

1. Marc Norman and Tom Stoppard, *Shakespeare in Love: A Screenplay* (New York: Hyperion, 1998), p. 147.

is divided into eight groups, each beginning with trumpeters, heralds, and banners. Among them, all of England is represented.

The final group begins with the Great Banner of England, carried by the earl of Pembroke and Charles Lord Howard of Effingham (the victor over the Armada). Then come the principal members of the College of Heralds (including the great historian William Camden) bearing the royal helmet, shield, sword, and coat of armor, just as if Elizabeth had literally had "the heart and stomach of a king, and of a king of England too." Then comes the catafalque. Following are the royal palfrey without its rider. Acting as chief mourner was the marchioness of Northampton (wife to Henry Howard, earl of Northampton, who had written his "Dutifull defence" of women rulers), followed by countesses and viscountesses, earls' daughters, and maids of honor. Last is Sir Walter Raleigh, commanding the Queen's Guard, their pikes pointed down in the dust.

From Whitehall Palace to Westminster Abbey went the procession, where Elizabeth was interred amidst the kings of England. Her tomb, completed by James in 1606, was instantly a tourist site and continues to receive a stream of visitors to this day. By the

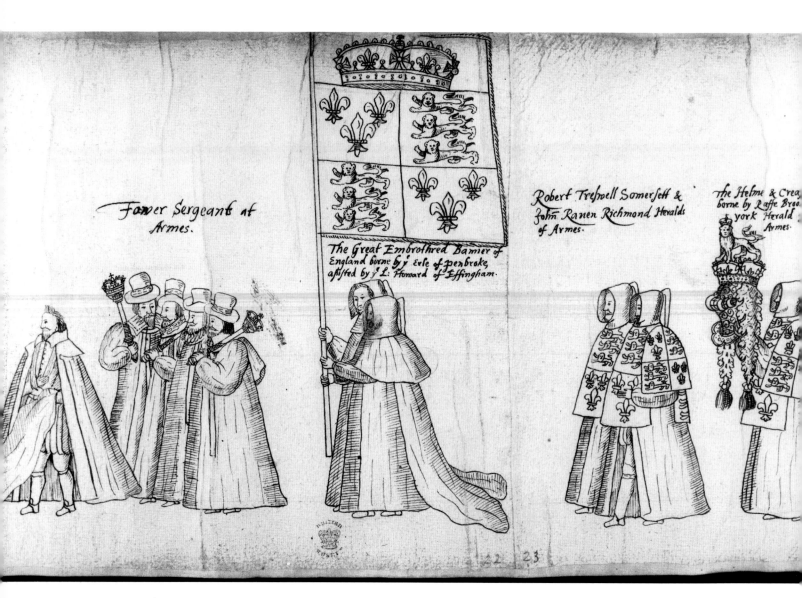

Fower Sergeants at
Armes.

The Great Embrothred Banner of
England borne by y Erle of penbroke,
assisted by y L: Howard of Effingham.

Robert Treswell Somersett &
John Ranen Richmond Heralds
of Armes.

the Helme & Crea
borne by Raffe Broo
york Herald
Armes.

FIGURE 94. Anonymous,
funeral procession of Elizabeth I, 1603 (detail). MS
Additional 5408. Repro-
duced by permission of the
British Library.

middle of the seventeenth century, engravings of the tomb were displayed in churches
throughout the country and were a feature of picture books showing the splendors of the
capital and the abbey (figure 98).

Still, the tomb has its ironies. James buried together the two Tudor half-sisters,
Elizabeth and Mary, in a chapel in the north ambulatory. (Fittingly, Elizabeth is on top.)
Opposite them on the south side he put his own mother, Mary Queen of Scots, as if she

The Charrett
wch Charrett ſtoo
veluet, & vppõ tha[t]
borne by 6· Knig[...]

borne by
as Cheſter
rmes.

The Sword borne by
William Seger Norroy
Kinge of Armes.

A Gentleman
uſher wth a
white rodd·

The Cote borne b[y]
william Camde[n]
Clarencieulp Kinge
of Armes.

A Gentleman
uſher wth a
white rode.

had been a monarch of England, and next to her, Margaret Stuart, countess of Lennox, the mother of James's father, Henry Stuart, Lord Darnley. In the middle of the chapel, next to Henry VII, he put his own tomb. The result is to create a central spine of tombs establishing James as the double descendent of Henry VII, via both Margaret Stuart and Mary Queen of Scots, and pushing Elizabeth and her siblings to the side, as if they were a digression. This is Elizabeth's final punishment for not having children of her own.

FIGURE 95. Anonymous, funeral procession of Elizabeth I, 1603 (detail). MS Additional 5408. Reproduced by permission of the British Library.

FIGURE 96. Anonymous,
funeral procession of Elizabeth I, 1603 (detail). MS
Additional 5408. Repro-
duced by permission of the
British Library.

The Erle of Worcester Mr of the
Horse Leading the palfrey of Estate. 2.
Esquires & a groome attending to Lead him
away.

A Gentleman Usher of the
priuy Chamber.

William Dethick Garter
principall Kinge of Armes.

The Lady Marchiones of
Northampton principall
mourner assisted by the Lord
Buckhurst Lord Treasurer & the
Erle of Nottingham Lord Admirall.

Her Trayne A
two Countesse
Stanhop vicech

FIGURE 97. Anonymous,
funeral procession of Elizabeth I, 1603 (detail). MS
Additional 5408. Repro-
duced by permission of the
British Library.

133

FIGURE 98. The tomb
of Elizabeth I, from John
Dart, *Westmonasterium*
(London, circa 1742).
Wing +W34455 .2,
vol. 1, p. 171. Newberry
Library, Chicago.

RULER AND LEGEND

Well before the death of Elizabeth, the historians were at work recording and assessing her reign. Indeed, Foxe's *Actes and Monuments*, published back in 1563, had begun the historiography of Elizabeth with its account of her "miraculous preservation" before coming to the throne. Later historians may be more reserved about the miracles, but they remain dependent on Foxe for collecting the accounts of early eye-witnesses.

Likewise the great William Camden had begun his work while Elizabeth was alive, but at the end of her reign, not the beginning. In 1597 Lord Burghley gave Camden access to his own and the queen's state papers. Over the next twenty years, Camden wove together a savvy insider's account of the politics of the reign. It is very much told from the point of view of Elizabeth's chief ministers and occasionally reflects their frustration with her when they don't get their way. But even Camden is not immune to her spellbinding qualities, and the contagion is reflected in the earliest publications of his work. The first edition of his *Annales of Queen Elizabeth*, published in Latin in 1615, uses as its frontispiece Francis Delaram's engraving of Elizabeth crowned in stars (see figure 1).

The first English edition, published in 1625 just after Camden's death, glories her even further (figure 99). The title itself has now become *Annales: The True and Royall History of the famous Empresse Elizabeth.* Surrounding the title is a massive triumphal arch on which are hung the arms of the leading figures of her reign. At the four corners are great accomplishments: raids on the Spanish at the top and Drake's voyages at the

FIGURE 99. Title page from William Camden, *Annales: The True and Royall History of the famous Empresse Elizabeth Queene of England France and Ireland* (London, 1625). Case F 4549 .137. Newberry Library, Chicago.

bottom. Above the arch is the Tudor rose, crowned, and surmounted by a phoenix. This is one of Elizabeth's special symbols. There is only one phoenix at any time, and when it dies, it rises again from the flames of its funeral pyre. Hence the bird is mystical and chaste, like Elizabeth (or indeed, like Christ). And it is always the same, again like Elizabeth, whose motto "Semper eadem" appears on a ribbon.

The simple fact is that Elizabeth, well before her death, had become identified with England itself. Christopher Saxton's 1575 *Atlas of England and Wales* opens with a magnificent title page showing Elizabeth enthroned, surrounded by the symbols of cartographic art (figure 100). The famous "Ditchley" portrait of 1592 shows Elizabeth standing on the Saxton map of England. A remarkable anonymous woodcut map of the British Isles dating to 1594 places Elizabeth's portrait onto the surface of the map, surrounded by a genealogical tree (plate 10). (The copy illustrated here of this extremely rare map has contemporary color and has never before been published.) Finally, on the title page of Michael Drayton's remarkable poem *Poly-Olbion, or A chorographical description of tracts, rivers, mountains, forests, and other parts of this renowned isle of Great Britain* (1612), the figure of Elizabeth on her throne from Saxton has metamorphosed into a figure of England herself, bearing a scepter and cornucopia, with the land draped over her, and with Greek, Roman, Saxon, and Norman figures flanking her (figure 101).

Works of fiction also began instantly—with only the minimal dash of history in them, or none at all. The playwright and fiction writer Thomas Heywood started up an Elizabeth industry all his own, ranging from his 1613 play *If you know not me, You know no bodie: Or, The troubles of Queene Elizabeth* (see figure 17) to his massive prose work *Englands Elizabeth: Her Life and Troubles, During Her Minoritie, from the Cradle to the Crowne* (1631) (figure 102). And his works had competitors, ranging from Christopher Lever's *Queene Elizabeth Teares: or, Her resolute bearing the Christian Crosse, inflicted on her by the persecuting hands of Steven Gardner Bishop of Winchester, in the bloodie time of Queene Marie* (1607) to the anonymous *Courtnay Earl of Devonshire; or, the Troubles of the Princess Elizabeth. A Tragedy* (1705).

By the late seventeenth century, Elizabeth's love life became a subject of obsession in England and especially in France. *The Secret History of the Most Renowned Q. Elizabeth, and the E. of Essex* is the most famous of the absurd tattle-tale books, but not the last (figure 103). There is also *The Secret History of the Duke of Alancon and Q. Elizabeth: A True History* (1691), written in a crisp documentary style, and the *Secret Memoirs of Robert Dudley, Earl of Leicester* (1706). These in turn have inspired nineteenth-century operas and an endless stream of modern pulp fiction. Gaetano Donizetti especially liked Elizabethan materials, churning out *Elisabetta al Castello di Kenilworth* (1829), *Anna Bolena* (1830), *Maria Stuarda* (1834), and *Roberto Devereux, Conte di Essex* (1837).

FIGURE 100. Title page from Christopher Saxton, *Atlas of England and Wales* (London, 1579). Case +G 1045 .78. Newberry Library, Chicago.

POLY-OLBION

GREAT BRITAINE

By Michaell Drayton Esqr:

London printed for M. Lownes. I. Browne. I. Hestaue. I. Helme. I. Busbie. Sr. W. Hole

FIGURE 101. Title page from Michael Drayton, *Poly-Olbion* (London, 1612). Wing fZP 645 .H71. Newberry Library, Chicago.

FIGURE 102. Frontispiece from Thomas Heywood, *Englands Elizabeth Her Life and Troubles, During Her Minoritie, from the Cradle to the Crowne* (London, 1631). Case E5 .E43235. Newberry Library, Chicago.

In the last few decades, certainly the most important addition to the legend of Elizabeth has been through film and television. Before and during World War II, Flora Robson portrayed Elizabeth as the defender of English liberty (figure 104). In *The Private Lives of Elizabeth and Essex* (1939), Bette Davis created a bitterly emotional Elizabeth owing more to the "secret histories" than to the historical record (figure 105). Glenda Jackson's television *Elizabeth R* of the 1970s stuck closer to the facts, creating a tough and resourceful Elizabeth for a generation of modern viewers (figure 106).

More recently, two competing images of Elizabeth have emerged from two very different films. In *Shakespeare in Love*, directed by John Madden, an aging Elizabeth, played by Judi Dench, is herself cynical but can remember what it was like to be young and romantic (figure 107). She is low-brow, all-seeing, and engineers an ending that is correct, if not so very happy. In *Elizabeth*, directed by Shekhar Kapur, a young Elizabeth

FIGURE 104. Flora Robson as
Queen Elizabeth I in *Fire over
England,* directed by William K.
Howard, 1937. Image courtesy
of Photofest.

played by Cate Blanchett is not altogether prepared and not altogether eager to be on the
throne (figure 108). Surrounded by dangers, she gradually cuts loose of her advisors and
finds her own way, trading personal fulfillment for solitary power. The script reflects a
thorough combing of Camden and especially of Foxe for vivid anecdotes, and a careful
study of what Elizabethan England and the Elizabethan court would have looked like. The
film is notoriously inaccurate in historical details, but accurate about the atmosphere of
terror that pervaded the sixteenth century, and accurate in showing the insecurity of
Elizabeth's throne up until the execution of Norfolk in 1572.

Elizabeth remains instantly recognizable four hundred years after her death: the
slightly hooked nose, the long fingers, the extravagant clothing form a visual signature
that corresponds to the famous flourish of the signature "Elizabeth R." It is impossible
now to disentangle the threads of history and legend within this image of Elizabeth. Likewise it was impossible to disentangle the ruler from the woman in her own time. In each

FIGURE 105. Bette Davis as Queen Elizabeth I in *The Private Lives of Elizabeth and Essex,* directed by Michael Curtiz, 1939. Image courtesy of Photofest.

FIGURE 106. Glenda Jackson as Queen Elizabeth I in *Elizabeth R,* directed by Roderick Graham, 1971. Image courtesy of Photofest.

FIGURE 107. Judi Dench as Queen Elizabeth I in *Shakespeare in Love,* directed by John Madden, 1998. Image courtesy of Photofest.

case, it is not because there is only the image and no "real" Elizabeth. Nor is it because the "real" Elizabeth was some inner secret and everything else an outward mask. Elizabeth was a figure of many controversies, and those controversies reflect the same questions that interest us now. Can a woman rule? What is the place of religion in the state? What is the price of peace or the true cause of war? What are the workings of political image-making itself? In each of these questions, the workings of history and legend are intertwined, and in each of these questions, the ruler both shapes and is shaped by them. Elizabeth cannot be separated from the legend that she helped to create.

FIGURE 108. Cate Blanchett
as Queen Elizabeth I in
Elizabeth, directed by
Shekhar Kapur, 1998.
Image courtesy of Photofest.

1. William Camden, *The Historie of the Most Renowned and Victorious Princess Elizabeth, Late Queen of England* (London, 1630), book 4, p. 224.
2. Ibid., p. 223.
3. Ibid.
4. Ibid.
5. William Shakespeare, *Henry VIII,* 5.4.25–37, in *The Norton Shakespeare,* ed. Stephen Greenblatt et al. (New York: Norton, 1997).
6. Clement Marot, "Le Pasteur évangelique," British Library, MS Royal 16 E. XIII, fol. 2r.
7. Queen Anne Boleyn to Lord Cobham, September 7, 1533, British Library, MS Harley 283, fol. 75r.
8. Roger Ascham to Johann Sturm, April 4, 1550, in *The Whole Works of Roger Ascham,* ed. J. A. Giles (1865; reprint, New York: AMS Press, 1965), vol. 1, p. lxiii.
9. David Starkey, *Elizabeth: Apprenticeship* (London: Vintage, 2000), pp. 81–85.
10. Edward Hall [and Richard Grafton], *The Union of the Two Noble and Illustrious Families of Lancaster and York* (London, 1548), p. 865.
11. Sir Robert Naunton, *Fragmenta Regalia, or Observations on The Late Queen Elizabeth, Her Times and Favorites* (London, 1641), fol. A3r.
12. Diana Scarisbrick, *Tudor and Jacobean Jewellry* (London: Tate, 1995), pp. 90–91.
13. Princess Elizabeth to Edward Seymour, Lord Protector, January 28, 1549, Hatfield House, Cecil Papers 133/4/2, *Elizabeth I: Collected Works,* ed. Leah S. Marcus, Janel Mueller, and Mary Beth Rose (Chicago: University of Chicago Press, 2000), p. 24.
14. Princess Elizabeth to Edward Seymour, Lord Protector, February 21, 1549, British Library, MS Lansdowne 1236, fol. 33r, *Elizabeth I: Collected Works,* p. 32.
15. Princess Elizabeth to King Edward VI, May 15, 1549, British Library, MS Cotton Vespasian F.III, fol. 48, *Elizabeth I: Collected Works,* p. 35.
16. John Aylmer, *An [Harbor] for Faithfull and Trewe Subjectes, agaynst the late blowne blaste, concerninge the Government of Wemen* (Strasbourg [London], 1559), fol. Nv.

17. Queen Jane [Grey] to William Parr, Marquis of Northampton, July 10, 1553, British Library, MS Lansdowne 1236, item 15, fol. 24.

18. John Foxe's work was written during the reign of Mary. The Latin version was first published in Basel, Switzerland, in 1559 (just as Elizabeth came to the throne), under the title *Rerum in ecclesia gestarum comentarii.* The English version was published in 1563 with the title *Actes and Monuments,* by which the work is usually known.

19. Queen Elizabeth to the Joint Delegation of Lords and Commons, November 5, 1566, version 2, Syndics of Cambridge University Library, MS Gg.III.34, fols. 208–12, *Elizabeth I: Collected Works,* p. 96.

20. Queen Elizabeth to the Lords and Councilors, November 20, 1558, PRO, State Papers Domestic, Elizabeth 12/1/7, *Elizabeth I: Collected Works,* p. 52.

21. [John Knox], *The First Blast of the Trumpet Against the Monstrous Regiment of Women* (Geneva, 1558), fol. Br.

22. Ibid., fol. G3r.

23. Ibid., fols. B2v–B3r.

24. Jeronymo da Fonseca Osorio, *An Epistle of the Reverend Father in God Hieronimos Osorios Bishop of Archburge in Portugale, to the most excellent Princesse Elizabeth by the grace of God Quene of England, Fraunce, and Ireland* ["A Pearle for a Prynce"] (Antwerp, 1565), p. 8r.

25. The text is from the "Bishops Bible" (London, 1568), the official Bible of the Elizabethan church.

26. John N. King, *Tudor Royal Iconography: Literature and Art in an Age of Religious Crisis* (Princeton: Princeton University Press, 1989), p. 154.

27. Archbishop Edmund Grindal to Elizabeth, December 20, 1576, *The Remains of Edmund Grindal, D.D.,* ed. William Nicholson (Cambridge: University Press, 1893), p. 389.

28. Guzman de Silva to the King, April 26, 1565, *Calendar of Letters and State Papers Relating to English Affairs Preserved in the Archives of Simancas* [State Papers Spanish], ed. Martin A. S. Hume (London, 1892–99), vol. 1, p. 425.

29. See Samuel P. Huntington, "The Clash of Civilizations?" *Foreign Affairs* 72 (Summer 1993): 22–49.

30. Bull of Pope Pius V, excommunicating Queen Elizabeth, February 25, 1570, *Calendar of State Papers and Manuscripts Relating to English Affairs Existing in the Archives and Collections of Venice,* ed. Rawdon Brown and G. Cavendish Bentinck (London, 1890), vol. 7, pp. 449–50.

31. William Camden, *The Historie of the Most Renowned and Victorious Princess Elizabeth,* 4th ed. (London, 1688), p. 18.

32. Sir Francis Bacon, "Certain Observations Made Upon a Libel Published this Present year, 1592," *The Letters and Life of Sir Francis Bacon,* ed. James Spedding (London: Longman, 1861), vol. 1, p. 178.

33. Eloy Koldeweij, *The English Candlestick, 1425–1925* (London: Christie's, 2001), cat. 4, p. 40.

34. The text is from the "Bishops Bible."

35. Queen Elizabeth to Parliament, February 10, 1559, version 1, British Library, MS Lansdowne 94, art. 14, fol. 29, *Elizabeth I: Collected Works,* p. 58.

36. Queen Elizabeth's Answer to the Commons' Petition, January 28, 1563, PRO, State Papers Domestic, Elizabeth 12/27/36, fols. 143r–144r, *Elizabeth I: Collected Works,* p. 72.

37. The Lords' Petition to Queen Elizabeth, circa February 1, 1563, PRO, State Papers Domestic, Elizabeth 12/27/35(A), fols. 135r–138v, *Elizabeth I: Collected Works,* pp. 81–82.

38. Queen Elizabeth's Answer to the Lords' Petition, April 10, 1563, British Library, MS Lansdowne 94, art. 15B, fol. 30r, *Elizabeth I: Collected Works,* pp. 79–80.

39. Queen Elizabeth to Joint Delegation, version 2, *Elizabeth I: Collected Works,* p. 95.

40. Queen Elizabeth to Parliament, January 2, 1567, version 1, British Library, MS Cotton Charter IV.38 (2), *Elizabeth I: Collected Works,* p. 105.

41. Queen Elizabeth to Parliament, January 2, 1567, version 2, British Library, MS Cotton Titus F.1., fols. 121v–122r, *Elizabeth I: Collected Works,* p. 107.

42. Anonymous, "A View, or Spectacle of Vanity," from Gabriel Harvey, autograph manuscript of a portion of a commonplace book (circa 1584), fol. 6, uncataloged, Rare Book and Special Collections Library, University of Illinois at Urbana-Champaign. See Alvan Bregman, "A Gabriel Harvey Manuscript Brought to Light," *The Book Collector* (forthcoming).

43. Naunton, *Fragmenta Regalia,* fol. A3v.

44. Sir James Melville, *The Memoirs of Sir James Melvil of HalHill* (Edinburgh, 1735), p. 96.

45. Carole Levin, *"The Heart and Stomach of a King": Elizabeth I and the Politics of Sex and Power* (Philadelphia: University of Pennsylvania Press, 1994), pp. 66–90.

46. Queen Elizabeth to Sir Thomas Smith and Dr. Thomas Wilson, September 16, 1571, British Library, MS Cotton Caligula C.III, fol. 242r, *Elizabeth I: Collected Works,* p. 127.

47. R.C. [Robert Cecil], *The Copie of a Letter to the Right Honourable the Earle of Leycester* (London, 1586), p. 14.

48. Ibid., p. 15.

49. Sir Robert Stafford to William Cecil, March 5, 1587, PRO, *Calendar of State Papers, Foreign Series, of the Reign of Elizabeth,* vol. 21, part 1, p. 236.

50. King James VI of Scotland to Queen Elizabeth, March 1587, British Library, MS Additional 23240, art. 20, fol. 65r, *Elizabeth I: Collected Works,* p. 297.

51. Robert Devereux, Earl of Essex, to Queen Elizabeth, October–November 1597, British Library, MS Additional 74286, fol. 99, #36.

52. John Nichols, *The Progresses and Public Processions of Queen Elizabeth* (London, 1823), vol. 3, p. 552.

53. Francis Bacon, *Sir Francis Bacon His Apologie, In Certaine Imputations concerning the late Earle of Essex* (London, 1605), p. 69.

54. Queen Elizabeth to the Troops at Tilbury, August 9, 1588, British Library, MS Harley 6798, art. 18, fol. 87 (author's transcription; cf. *Elizabeth I: Collected Works,* pp. 325–26).

55. Queen Elizabeth to King James VI of Scotland, January 1593, British Library, MS Additional 23240, art. 32, fols. 108r–109r, *Elizabeth I: Collected Works,* p. 366.

56. Ibid., p. 368.

57. Jean de Beauchesne, calligraphy book for Princess Elizabeth (circa 1610), Newberry Library, Wing MS ZW 639 .B382, fol. Br.

58. Thomas Newton, *Atropoïon Delion, Or, The death of Delia: With the Teares of her Funerall. A Pöeticall Excusive Discourse of our late Eliza* (London, 1603), fol. B2v.

59. Thomas Smith, *Sir Thomas Smithes Voiage and Entertainment in Rushia* (London, 1605), fols. Fv–F2r.

EXHIBITION CHECKLIST

Asterisks indicate items included in the American Library Association exhibition.

THE YOUNG ELIZABETH

*Circle of Quentin Massys the Younger, *Sieve Portrait of Queen Elizabeth I* (circa 1580–83). Oil on panel. 112 × 79.5 cm. Mr. and Mrs. John H. Bryan.

*William Shakespeare, *Mr. William Shakespeares Comedies, Histories, & Tragedies* (London, 1623). Newberry Library, Chicago (Case YS 01).

*Henry VIII, grant to Roland Babington of the manor of Normanton, Westminster (November 22, 1544). Kenneth Spencer Research Library, MS J35. University of Kansas, Lawrence.

Elizabeth I, instrument of recovery of the manor of Brantingsten, with Royal Seal (1579). Newberry Library, Chicago (Wing MS +ZW 1.579).

*"Italian Motets and Madrigals: Henry VIII Part Books" (circa 1527–28). Newberry Library, Chicago (Case MS VM 1578 M91).

*The Malmsbury-Caird Cup (1529). Silver-gilt standing cup. Height 21.5 cm. Mr. and Mrs. John H. Bryan.

Clement Marot, "Le Pasteur évangelique" [The evangelical shepherd] (1533). British Library, London (MS Royal 16 E. XIII).

Queen Anne Boleyn, birth announcement for a "princes," to George Brooke, Lord Cobham (September 7, 1533). British Library, London (MS Harley 283, fol. 75r).

Nicholas Sander, *De Origine Ac Progressu Schismatis Anglicani* [History of the schism in the English church] (Cologne, 1585). Newberry Library, Chicago (Case 3A 1513).

Gentleman's embroidered nightcap (circa 1600). Red and green silk, silver-gilt thread, sequins, and gold lace on linen. Mr. and Mrs. John H. Bryan.

*After Hans Holbein the Younger, *Anne Boleyn* (late nineteenth century). Tempera on ivory. 9 × 7 cm. Private collection.

Princess Elizabeth, letter to Edward Seymour, Lord Protector (February 21, 1549). British Library, London (MS Lansdowne 1236, fol. 33r).

Queen Jane [Grey], letter to William Parr, Marquis of Northampton (July 10, 1553). British Library, London (MS Lansdowne 1236, item 15, fol. 24r).

*John Foxe, *Actes and Monuments* (London, 1583). Newberry Library, Chicago (Case fD78 .308).

Roger Ascham, *The Scholemaster Or plaine and perfite way of teaching children* (London, 1571). Newberry Library, Chicago (Case I 4 .047, no. 2).

*Robert Cooke, "Armorial bearings of the kings and noble families of Great Britain from the reign of William the Conqueror to that of James I" (1572). Newberry Library, Chicago (Case MS F 0745 .1915).

Sixtus ab Hemminga, *Astrologiæ* (Antwerp, 1583). Newberry Library, Chicago (Case B8635 .386).

*William Scrots (attributed), *Elizabeth I when Princess* (circa 1546–47). Oil on panel. 108.8 × 81.9 cm. Royal Collection. (Photographic reproduction)

ELIZABETH THE QUEEN

Drawings for the entry into London of Elizabeth I (1558). British Library, London (MS Egerton 3320, fols. 4v–5r).

*Elizabeth I, appointment of Edward North as Lord Lieutenant of Cambridgeshire and the Isle of Ely (May 1, 1559). Kenneth Spencer Research Library, MS J36. University of Kansas, Lawrence.

*Elizabethan sixpence coin (1581). Private collection.

*Anonymous, *Elizabeth I* (circa 1564–67). Oil on panel. 35.6 × 22.9 cm. Mr. and Mrs. John H. Bryan.

*John Knox, *The First Blast of the Trumpet Against the Monstrous Regimen of Women* (Philadelphia, 1766). Newberry Library, Chicago (Case oJN 1239 1766 .B8, no. 2).

John Aylmer, *An [Harbor] for Faithfull and Trewe Subjectes, agaynst the late blowne blaste, concerninge the Government of Wemen* (Strasbourg [London], 1559). Newberry Library, Chicago (Case K771 .468).

Henry Howard, "A dutifull defence of the lawfull regiment of women" (1589). Newberry Library, Chicago (Case MS fJ 5452 .634).

*John Case, *Sphæra Civitatis* [The sphere of state] (Oxford, 1588). Newberry Library, Chicago (Case JO .148).

*Elizabeth I, answer to the Lords' petition that she marry (April 10, 1563). British Library, London (MS Lansdowne 94, art. 15B, fol. 30r).

Elizabeth I, speech dissolving Parliament (January 2, 1567). British Library, London (MS Cotton Charter IV.38 [2]).

*After François Clouet, *Duc d'Alençon,* from Frederick Chamberlain, *The Sayings of Queen Elizabeth* (London: John Lane, 1923). Newberry Library, Chicago (E5 .E43204). (Photographic reproduction)

*Nicholas Hilliard, *Robert Dudley, Earl of Leicester* (1576). Ink and color on card. Diameter 4.5 cm. National Portrait Gallery, London. (Photographic reproduction)

John Stubbs, *The Discoverie of a Gaping Gulf Whereinto England is Like to be Swallowed by an other French mariage, if the Lord forbid not the banes, by letting her Majestie see the sin and punishment thereof* (N.p., 1579). Newberry Library, Chicago (Case 3A .2106).

Elizabeth I, letter to Catherine de Medici on the death of Duc d'Alençon (circa July 1584). British Library, London (MS Cotton Galba E. VI, fol. 255r).

Gabriel Harvey, commonplace book (circa 1584). Rare Book and Special Collections Library, University of Illinois at Urbana-Champaign (uncataloged).

Thomas Rogers, "The Earle of Leicesters Ghoste" (circa 1602–4). Newberry Library, Chicago (Case MS Y185 .L53).

*Sheldon Tapestry Works, Barcheston, England. "Susanna and the Elders" (circa 1600). Colored wools and silks with metallic threads. 55.9 × 104.1 cm. Mr. and Mrs. John H. Bryan.

*_The holie Bible. conteynyng the olde Testament and the newe_ ["Bishops Bible"] (London, 1568). Newberry Library, Chicago (Case +C221 .568).

The Booke of Common prayer (London, 1577). Newberry Library, Chicago (Case C8726 .577).

Church of England, _Articles to be enquired in the visitation, in the firste yere of the raigne of our moste dread Soveraigne Lady, Elizabeth by the grace of God, of Englande, Fraunce, and Irelande, Queene, defendour of the faith_ (London, 1559). Newberry Library, Chicago (Wing ZP 545 .J93).

Brass candlestick (circa 1500–1550). 17.5 × 11.4 cm. Mr. and Mrs. John H. Bryan.

*The burning of John Hooper, bishop at Gloucester, from John Foxe, _Actes and Monuments_ (London, 1583). Newberry Library, Chicago (Case fD78 .308, p. 1510). (Photographic reproduction)

*The persecution of Catholics in Ireland, from Richard Verstegen, _Theatrum Crudelitatum Hæreticorum Nostri Temporis_ [A theater of the cruelty of the heretics in our time] (Antwerp, 1592). Newberry Library, Chicago (Case D78 .938, p. 81). (Photographic reproduction)

Jeronymo da Fonseca Osorio, _An Epistle of the Reverend Father in God Hieronimos Osorios Bishop of Archburge in Portugale, to the most excellent Princesse Elizabeth by the grace of God Quene of England, Fraunce, and Ireland_ ["A Pearle for a Prynce"] (Antwerp, 1565). Newberry Library, Chicago (Case C64 .6468).

The Bible and Holy Scriptures Conteyned in the Olde and Newe Testament ["Geneva Bible"] (Geneva, 1560). Newberry Library, Chicago (Case C22 .560).

*Richard Day, _A booke of christian prayers_ ["The Queen's Prayerbook"] (London, 1581). Rare Book and Special Collections Library, University of Illinois at Urbana-Champaign (248 D33b 1581).

Needlework dos-à-dos binding (circa 1638) for the Book of Psalms (London, 1628) and the New Testament (London, 1638). Private collection.

*Thomas Barlow, _Brutum Fulmen: or the Bull of Pope Pius V. Concerning the Damnation, Excommunication, and Deposition of Q. Elizabeth_ (London, 1681). Newberry Library, Chicago (Case C764 .072). (Photographic reproduction)

SEDITION AND SUCCESSION

William Fleetwood, _The effect of the declaration made in the Guildhall by M. Recorder of London, concerning the late attemptes of the Quenes Majesties evill, seditious, and disobedient subjectes_ (London, 1571). Newberry Library, Chicago (Case F4549 .303).

Claude, Lord Nau, letter to Robert Beale concerning Mary Queen of Scots (1582). Newberry Library, Chicago (Case MS 5091).

R.C. [Robert Cecil], *The Copie of a Letter to the Right Honourable the Earle of Leycester* (London, 1586). Newberry Library, Chicago (Case DA 787 .A2 S2 1586).

Elizabeth I, speech to Parliament concerning Mary Queen of Scots (November 12, 1586). British Library, London (MS Lansdowne 94, art. 35A, fols. 84r–85r).

*After François Clouet, *Mary Queen of Scots* (late nineteenth century). Tempera on ivory. 5 × 4 cm. Newberry Library, Chicago (Case oDA787 .A3 .P7, no. 1).

Oak armchair with arms of the Arundel family (circa 1570). Height 101.5 cm. Mr. and Mrs. John H. Bryan.

Robert Beale, drawing of the execution of Mary Queen of Scots (1587). British Library, London (MS Additional 48027, fol. 650).

Henry Grey, Earl of Kent, letter to William Cecil, Lord Burghley (copy by Robert Beale). Description of the execution of Mary Queen of Scots (February 8, 1587). Newberry Library, Chicago (Case MS 5089).

*James VI of Scotland, letter to Elizabeth I regarding the execution of Mary Queen of Scots (March 1587). British Library, London (MS Additional 23240, art. 20, fol. 65r).

Robert Devereux, Earl of Essex, letter to Elizabeth I (October–November 1597). British Library, London (MS Additional 74286, fol. 99, #36).

*Francis Jobson, map of Ulster (circa 1590). British Library, London (MS Cotton Augustus I. ii. 19).

John Hayward, *The First Part of the Life and raigne of King Henrie the IIII* (London, 1599). Newberry Library, Chicago (Case F4536 .39).

*Francis Bacon, *A Declaration of the Practices & Treasons attempted and committed by Robert late Earle of Essex and his Complices* (London, 1601). Newberry Library, Chicago (Case F4549 .268).

Francis Bacon, *Sir Francis Bacon His Apologie, In Certaine Imputations concerning the late Earle of Essex* (London, 1605). Newberry Library, Chicago (Case -E5 .E7862).

*John Leslie, *De Titulo et Jure Serenissimæ Principis Mariæ Scotorum Reginæ, quo Regni Angliæ Successionem sibi justè vendicat* [The title and right of Mary, most serene Queen of Scots, to the succession of the throne of England] (Rheims, 1580). Newberry Library, Chicago (Case 4A .1828).

R. Doleman [Robert Parsons], *A Conference About the Next Succession to the Crowne of Ingland* (Antwerp, 1594). Newberry Library, Chicago (Case 3A .1453).

John Hayward, *An Answer to the First Part of a Certaine Conference, Concerning Succession, Published not long since under the name of R. Dolman* (London, 1603). Newberry Library, Chicago (Case J 445 .668).

British School, *Henry VIII, Edward VI, and Elizabeth I* ["Professors and Defendors of the True Catholicke Faythe"] (1597). Oil on panel. 63 × 78 cm. Gift of Kate S. Buckingham, Art Institute of Chicago.

ELIZABETH'S ENGLAND

*Christopher Saxton, *Atlas of England and Wales* (London, 1579). Newberry Library, Chicago (Case +G 1045 .78).

Michael Drayton, *Poly-Olbion* (London, 1612). Newberry Library, Chicago (Wing fZP 645 .H71).

Anonymous, after Jodocus Hondius, map of England, Wales, and Ireland with genealogy and portrait of Queen Elizabeth I (1594). Engraving with color. 43 × 58.5 cm. Private collection.

*William Cuningham, *The Cosmographical Glasse* (London, 1559). Newberry Library, Chicago (Wing fZP545 .D27).

John Norden, *Speculum Britanniae* (London, 1593). Newberry Library, Chicago (Case G45004 .6).

Diego Homem, "Queen Mary Atlas" (1558). British Library, London (MS Additional 5415A, fols. 9v–10r).

*Cesare Vecellio, *Habiti Antichi, et Moderni di tutto il Mondo* [Ancient and modern costumes of the world] (Venice, 1598). Newberry Library, Chicago (Ayer *335 .V3 1598). (Photographic reproduction)

*Georg Braun and Franz Hogenberg, *Civitatis Orbis Terrarum* [Cities of the world] (Cologne, 1577). Newberry Library, Chicago (Ayer *135 B8 .1573, vols. 1–3).

Thomas Tallis and William Byrd, *Cantiones, quae ab argumento sacrae vocantur* [Songs called sacred because of their texts] (London, 1575). Newberry Library, Chicago (Case -VM 2099 L63 T14c).

*William Byrd, *Psalmes, sonets, & songs of sadnes and pietie* (London, circa 1590). Newberry Library, Chicago (Case -VM 1579 .B99p).

Gabriel Harvey's copy of Thomas Hoby, *The Courtyer of Count Baldessar Castilio* (London, 1561). Newberry Library, Chicago (Case Y712 .C27495).

Thomas Wilson, *The rule of Reason, conteinyng the Arte of Logique* (London, 1551). Newberry Library, Chicago (Case B49 .976).

*John Scottowe, "Calligraphic Alphabet" (1592). Newberry Library, Chicago (Wing MS ZW 545 .S431).

Esther Inglish, "A New Yeeres Guift" (1606–7). Newberry Library, Chicago (Wing MS ZW 645 .K29).

[George Puttenham], *The Arte of English Poesie* (London, 1589). Newberry Library, Chicago (Case YO4 .719).

*"Aprill," woodcut from Edmund Spenser, *The Shepheardes Calendar* (London, 1581). Newberry Library, Chicago (Case 3A .675). (Photographic reproduction)

Edmund Spenser, *The Faerie Queene* (London, 1590). Newberry Library, Chicago (Case 4A .923, vol. 1).

William Alabaster, "Elisæis" (circa 1591). Newberry Library, Chicago (Case MS Y.682 .A3).

*William Shakespeare, *A Pleasant Conceited Comedie Called, Loves labors lost* (London, 1598). Newberry Library, Chicago (Case 4A .949).

Thomas Heywood, *If you know not me, You know no bodie: Or, The troubles of Queene Elizabeth* (London, 1613). Newberry Library, Chicago (Case 4A .881).

*Ro. La. [Robert Laneham], *A Letter: Whearein, part of the entertainment untoo the Queens Majesty, at Killingwoorth Castl, in Warwik Sheer in this Soomers Progress 1575. is signified* (London, 1575). Newberry Library, Chicago (Case F4549 .478).

George Gascoigne, *The Whole woorkes of George Gascoigne* (London, 1587). Newberry Library, Chicago (Case Y 12 .G208).

Sir Walter Scott, *Kenilworth; A Romance* (Edinburgh, 1821). Newberry Library, Chicago (Y155.S 454, vols. 1–3).

*German ceramic jug from Littlecote House, with arms of Elizabeth I (1594). Stoneware. Height 35.6 cm. Mr. and Mrs. John H. Bryan.

John Nichols, *The Progresses and Public Processions of Queen Elizabeth* (London, 1823). Newberry Library, Chicago (Case F4549 .626, vol. 1).

EUROPE AND AMERICA

Christopher Saxton, proof sheet of "Northumberland," annotated by William Cecil, Lord Burghley (1575). British Library, London (MS Royal 18 D. III, fols. 71v–72r).

Robert Adams, "Thamesis Descriptio" (1588). British Library, London (MS Additional 44839).

Elizabeth I, speech to English troops at Tilbury (August 9, 1588). British Library, London (MS Harley 6798, art. 18, fol. 87r).

Pedro de Ribadeneyra, *Hystoria Ecclesiastica del scisma del Reyno de Inglaterra* [The ecclesiastical history of the schism of the realm of England] (Lisbon, 1588). Newberry Library, Chicago (Case oBR 375 .R52 1588).

A Packe of Spanish Lyes, Sent Abroad in the World: First printed in Spaine in the Spanish tongue, and translated out of the Originall. Now ripped up, unfolded, and by just examination condemned, as conteyning false, corrupt, and detestable wares, worthy to be damned and burned (London, 1588). Newberry Library, Chicago (Ayer *150.3 E7 P11 1588).

*John Pine, after Cornelius Vroom, "The Spanish and English Fleets off the Isle of Portland." *The Engravings of the Hangings of the House of Lords* (London, 1739; reprinted London, 1919). Newberry Library, Chicago (Case Y 008 .76, plate 5). (Photographic reproduction)

*Baptista Boazio, map of "The famouse West Indian voyadge" (1589). Engraving with color. 41 × 53 cm. Newberry Library, Chicago (Ayer *133 .D7 .B66 1589).

*Jodocus Hondius, "Vera Totius Expeditionis Nauticae" [An accurate description of the voyage around the world of Sir Francis Drake] (circa 1595). Engraving. 38.5 × 54.5 cm. Arthur Holzheimer Collection.

*Thomas Hariot, *A briefe and true report of the new found land of Virginia* (Frankfurt, 1590). Newberry Library, Chicago (Ayer *f150.5 V7 H2 1590).

*Walter Raleigh, *The Discoverie of Guiana* (Nürnberg, 1598). Newberry Library, Chicago (Case G985 .732).

Theodor De Bry, *Brevis Narratio . . . Americæ* [Brief narration . . . of America] (Frankfurt, 1590). Newberry Library, Chicago (Ayer *110 .B9 1590a, vol. 2). (Photographic reproduction)

*Robert Peake (attributed), *Queen Elizabeth I Being Carried in Procession* (circa 1600). Oil on canvas. 132 × 190.5 cm. Private collection/Bridgeman Art Library. (Photographic reproduction)

LEGACY AND LEGEND

Elizabeth I, letter to James VI of Scotland (January 1593). British Library, London (MS Additional 23240, art. 32, fols. 108r–109r).

*Anonymous, funeral procession of Elizabeth I (1603). British Library, London (MS Additional 5408).

Thomas Newton, *Atropoïon Delion, Or, The death of Delia: With the Teares of her Funerall. A Pöeticall Excusive Discourse of our late Eliza* (London, 1603). Newberry Library, Chicago (Case 4A .911).

Thomas Smith, *Sir Thomas Smithes Voiage and Entertainment in Rushia* (London, 1605). Newberry Library, Chicago (Case F541 .826).

*John Dart, *Westmonasterium* (London, circa 1742). Newberry Library, Chicago (Wing +W34455 .2, vol. 1).

*Nicholas Hilliard, *James I* (circa 1610). Ink and color on vellum. Diameter 4.5 cm. Mr. and Mrs. John H. Bryan.

Gilbert Dugdale, *Discours Triomphal* (Rouen, 1604). Newberry Library, Chicago (Case F39 .326 1604du).

Jean de Beauchesne, "A Madame Elizabeth, fille unique du Roy de la grand Bretaigne" [Calligraphy book for Princess Elizabeth Stuart] (circa 1610). Newberry Library, Chicago (Wing MS ZW 639 .B382).

*William Camden, *Annales: The True and Royall History of the famous Empresse Elizabeth Queene of England France and Ireland* (London, 1625). Newberry Library, Chicago (Case F 4549 .137).

Simonds D'Ewes, *A Compleat Journal of the Votes, Speeches and Debates, both of the House of Lords and House of Commons Throughout the whole Reign of Queen Elizabeth, Of Glorious Memory* (London, 1693). Newberry Library, Chicago (Case fK 1454 .231).

The Secret History of the Duke of Alancon and Q. Elizabeth: A True History (London, 1691). Newberry Library, Chicago (Case Y 1565 .S4664).

The Secret History of the Most Renowned Q. Elizabeth, and the E. of Essex (Cologne, 1680). Newberry Library, Chicago (Case Y1565 .S4674).

Secret Memoirs of Robert Dudley, Earl of Leicester, Prime Minister and Favourite of Queen Elizabeth (London, 1706). Newberry Library, Chicago (E5 L 5328).

John Neale, *Elizabeth I and Her Parliaments, 1559–1581* (London: J. Cape, 1953). Newberry Library, Chicago (K 0455 .615).

Carole Levin, *"The Heart and Stomach of a King": Elizabeth I and the Politics of Sex and Power* (Philadelphia: University of Pennsylvania Press, 1994). Private collection.

Leah S. Marcus, Janel Mueller, and Mary Beth Rose, eds., *Elizabeth I: Collected Works* (Chicago: University of Chicago Press, 2000). Private collection.

David Starkey, *Elizabeth: Apprenticeship* (London: Chatto and Windus, 2000). Private collection.

Giles Milton, *Big Chief Elizabeth: The Adventures and Fate of the First English Colonists in America* (New York: Picador, 2001). Private collection.

Alan Axelrod, *Elizabeth I, CEO: Strategic Lessons from the Leader Who Built an Empire* (Paramus, N.J.: Prentice Hall, 2000). Private collection.

*Ally Sheedy and Jessica Ann Levy, *She Was Nice to Mice* (New York: McGraw-Hill, 1975). Private collection.

Robin Maxwell, *The Queen's Bastard* (New York: Simon and Schuster, 2000). Private collection.

Flora Robson as Queen Elizabeth I in *Fire over England* (1937). Photograph.

Bette Davis as Queen Elizabeth I in *The Private Lives of Elizabeth and Essex* (1939). Photograph.

*Glenda Jackson as Queen Elizabeth I in *Elizabeth R* (1971). Photograph.

*Judi Dench as Queen Elizabeth I in *Shakespeare in Love* (1998). Photograph.

*Cate Blanchett as Queen Elizabeth I in *Elizabeth* (1998). Photograph.

SUGGESTED READING

Camden, William. *The History of the Most Renowned and Victorious Princess Elizabeth, Late Queen of England* [1625]. Edited by Wallace T. MacCaffrey. Chicago: University of Chicago Press, 1970.

Chinnery, Victor. *Oak Furniture: The British Tradition: A History of Early Furniture in the British Isles and New England.* Woodbridge, Eng.: Antique Collectors' Club, 1979.

Cole, Mary Hill. *The Portable Queen: Elizabeth I and the Politics of Ceremony.* Amherst: University of Massachusetts Press, 1999.

Collinson, Patrick. *The Religion of the Protestants.* Oxford: Clarendon, 1982.

Dixon, Annette, ed. *Women Who Ruled: Queens, Goddesses, Amazons in Renaissance and Baroque Art.* London: Merrell, 2002.

Dobson, Michael, and Nicola J. Watson. *England's Elizabeth: An Afterlife in Fame and Fantasy.* Oxford: Oxford University Press, 2002.

Doran, Susan. *Elizabeth: The Exhibition at the National Maritime Museum.* London: Chatto and Windus, 2003.

Frye, Susan. *Elizabeth I: The Competition for Representation.* New York: Oxford University Press, 1993.

Gurr, Andrew. *Playgoing in Shakespeare's London.* 2d ed. Cambridge: Cambridge University Press, 1996.

Guy, John. *The Reign of Elizabeth I: Court and Culture in the Last Decade.* Cambridge: Cambridge University Press, 1995.

———. *Tudor England.* Oxford: Oxford University Press, 1988.

Haigh, Christopher. *Elizabeth I.* 2d ed. Harlow: Longman, 1998.

———, ed. *The Reign of Elizabeth I.* Basingstoke: Macmillan, 1984.

Harvey, P. D. A. *Maps in Tudor England.* London: Public Record Office and the British Library, 1993.

Howarth, David. *Images of Rule: Art and Politics in the English Renaissance, 1485–1649.* Berkeley: University of California Press, 1997.

Jordan, Constance. *Renaissance Feminism: Literary Texts and Political Models.* Ithaca, N.Y.: Cornell University Press, 1990.

King, John N. *Tudor Royal Iconography: Literature and Art in an Age of Religious Crisis.* Princeton: Princeton University Press, 1989.

Levin, Carole. *"The Heart and Stomach of a King": Elizabeth I and the Politics of Sex and Power.* Philadelphia: University of Pennsylvania Press, 1994.

———. *The Reign of Elizabeth I.* New York: Palgrave, 2002.

MacCaffrey, Wallace T. *Elizabeth I.* London: Edward Arnold, 1993.

———. *Queen Elizabeth and the Making of Policy, 1572–1588.* Princeton: Princeton University Press, 1981.

———. *The Shaping of the Elizabethan Regime.* Princeton: Princeton University Press, 1968.

Marcus, Leah S., and Janel Mueller, eds. *Elizabeth I: Autograph Compositions and Foreign Language Originals.* Chicago: University of Chicago Press, 2003.

Marcus, Leah S., Janel Mueller, and Mary Beth Rose, eds. *Elizabeth I: Collected Works.* Chicago: University of Chicago Press, 2000.

Neale, J. E. *Elizabeth I and Her Parliaments.* 2 vols. London: J. Cape, 1953–57.

———. *Queen Elizabeth.* London: J. Cape, 1938.

Nichols, John. *The Progresses and Public Processions of Queen Elizabeth.* 3 vols. 1823. Reprint, New York: AMS Press, 1961.

Scarisbrick, Diana. *Tudor and Jacobean Jewellery.* London: Tate, 1995.

Scarisbrick, J. J. *The Reformation and the English People.* Oxford: Blackwell, 1984.

Shirley, Rodney W. *Early Printed Maps of the British Isles, 1477–1650.* London: Map Collectors' Circle, 1973–74.

Somerset, Anne. *Elizabeth I.* New York: Knopf, 1991.

Starkey, David. *Elizabeth: The Struggle for the Throne.* New York: HarperCollins Publishers, 2001.

Strong, Roy. *The Cult of Elizabeth: Elizabethan Portraiture and Pageantry.* Berkeley: University of California Press, 1977.

———. *The English Icon: Elizabethan and Jacobean Portraiture.* New York: Pantheon Books, 1969.

———. *Gloriana.* New York: Thames and Hudson, 1987.

———. *Tudor and Jacobean Portraits.* 2 vols. London: Her Majesty's Stationery Office, 1969.

Thurley, Simon. *The Royal Palaces of Tudor England: Architecture and Court Life, 1460–1547.* New Haven: Yale University Press, 1993.

Walker, Julia M., ed. *Dissing Elizabeth: Negative Representations of Gloriana.* Durham: Duke University Press, 1998.

Warnicke, Retha M. *The Rise and Fall of Anne Boleyn: Family Politics at the Court of Henry VIII.* New York: Cambridge University Press, 1989.

Watkins, John. *Representing Elizabeth in Stuart England: Literature, History, Sovereignty.* Cambridge: Cambridge University Press, 2002.

Wells, Robin Headlam. *Spenser's* Faerie Queene *and the Cult of Elizabeth.* London: Croom Helm, 1983.

Wernham, R. B. *After the Armada: Elizabethan England and the Struggle for Western Europe, 1588–1595.* Oxford: Clarendon Press, 1983.

———. *Before the Armada: The Growth of English Foreign Policy, 1485–1588.* London: Cape, 1966.

Williams, Penry. *The Tudor Regime.* Oxford: Clarendon, 1979.

Wormald, Jenny. *Mary, Queen of Scots: Politics, Passion and a Kingdom Lost.* 1988. Reprint, London: Tauris Parke Paperbacks, 2001.

Yates, Frances A. *Astraea: The Imperial Theme in the Sixteenth Century.* London: Routledge and Kegan Paul, 1975.

Ziegler, Georgianna, ed. *Elizabeth I: Then and Now.* Seattle: University of Washington Press, 2003.

SUGGESTED READING

CLARK HULSE is the author of *The Rule of Art: Literature and Painting in the Renaissance* and *Metamorphic Verse: The Elizabethan Minor Epic*, and coeditor, with Peter Erickson, of *Early Modern Visual Culture: Representation, Race, and Empire in the English Renaissance.* He is executive vice provost and dean of the graduate college at the University of Illinois at Chicago.

The University of Illinois Press is a
founding member of the Association of
American University Presses.

The text is typeset in Filosofia, a historical revival
based on the work of Bodoni. It was designed by
Zuzanna Licko and published by Emigre. The sidebars
are typeset in Meta, designed by Erik Spiekermann
and published by FontFont. The display is typeset in
Charlemagne, designed by Carol Twombly and published by Adobe Systems, Inc. Charlemagne is based
on the versal capitals of late tenth-century England.

The book was designed by Copenhaver Cumpston with
assistance from Amber Pliler, typeset by Jim Proefrock,
and manufactured by Four Colour Imports, Ltd.

UNIVERSITY OF ILLINOIS PRESS
1325 South Oak Street   Champaign, IL 61820-6903
WWW.PRESS.UILLINOIS.EDU